Lavender

Lavender in nature and garden, home and kitchen

Text by Anne Simonet-Avril

Photography by Sophie Boussahba

Lavender

Lavender in nature and garden, home and kitchen

KUBIK
PUBLISHING RvR

First published 2005 under the title:
*Lavande. La lavande aux champs, au jardin,
dans la maison et dans l'assiette* by Kubik éditions
© Archipel studio, 2005

This edition © Kubik/RvR 2005
RvR Verlagsgesellschaft
Schulstraße 64, D–77694 Kehl, Germany
www.kubikinternational.de
ISBN: 3-938265-14-0

Printed in Spain, April 2005

PUBLISHER
Jean-Jacques Brisebarre

DESIGN
Thomas Brisebarre

LAYOUT
Emmanuelle Delebecque

English edition produced by
Silva Editions Ltd

PROJECT COORDINATION
Sylvia Goulding

TRANSLATOR
Jennifer Patterson

COPY EDITOR
Kate Bethell

Previous page: Lavandins coming into
flower at the end of June – their blue
colour is just beginning to show.

Above: Lavender field with stone
shelter at the Montagne de Lure.

Right: Bees working in harmony
with lavender.

Contents

The scents and colours of Provence

Left: Making decorative
bouquets of dried lavender.

Below: Eau de toilette label
from the beginning of the
twentieth century, showing
a marriage of Art Nouveau
and Art Deco styles.
(From the collection of
Lucien Vakanas)

"Thankfully, I am not one of those flowers that decorate the flowerbeds… I don't risk falling into vile hands and I am sheltered from frivolous gossip. Nature has dictated that I grow quite far from water, unlike my sister plants, so I do not frequent civilized places nor cultivated ground. I am wild. Set apart from civilization, I inhabit solitary, deserted places on arid ground. I do not like crowds. As I was neither sown nor cultivated, no one can blame me for the care that I have not received. Free… I am free."

This short extract from the 'Tale of the Girl Heart's-Miracle, Lieutenant of the Birds' from The Arabian Nights celebrates lavender – the wonderful, blue, flowering plant that previously grew only in hot, dry and remote places, far away from agrarian cultivation. A plant that even sheep would ignore, but a universal remedy with which the shepherds filled their pouches…

High up on top of the Provençal mountains, this wild plant existed in harmony with four particular animals: the ass which carried the old still for extracting perfume; the partridge which built its nest in the shelter of the clumps; the bee which searched out the coloured pollen on its stamens that scented the honey; and the hare which hid under the long stems of the plant as they waved in the breeze blown by the Mistral.

Perfume makers from the town of Grasse, attracted by the subtle floral, herbal fragrance of its flowers, were the first to think of cultivating lavender, transferring plants from the windy hilltops to more accessible plateaus. Here they multiplied, producing an infinite number of plants that cover dry stretches of ground with intense lavender blue and add to the gentle relief of the solitary hillsides that the writer Jean Giono used as the setting for his novels. Economically, this lavender blue is the

Provençal gold and has brought wealth to country folk who lived in extreme poverty due to the poor harvests of rye and spelt.

A new discovery

The incomparably beautiful countryside where lavender grows remained, for a long time, unknown to the general public and was scorned by artists. One of the first to pay homage to it was the writer Jean Giono. The simple opening sentences of this short passage still ring true today:

"Lavender is the very soul of Haute Provence. Whether one arrives from the Drôme, from Dauphiné or from the Var, the earth here stretches out, an empty arid expanse covered in violet hues and wonderfully scented…"

In the past, visitors to the South of France usually stayed around the Riviera on the Côte d'Azur, where the gardens are a paradise filled with orange and lemon trees, bordered by palm trees and oleanders. Gradually, however, growing crowds on the beaches and urban expansion on the coast drove those searching for a more authentic experience towards Haute Provence, up into the interior of a secret country, where lavender-blue fields stretch as far as the eye can see, filling the holidays with scented memories and flowers. By the end of the twentieth century, lavender had become both the visual and the olfactory symbol of Provence. Little by little, this wild mountain flower had been tamed by the modern world. By including it as an ingredient in various eau de Colognes and in many other fragrances, perfume makers bestowed status upon it. Even the French emperor, Napoleon Bonaparte, washed and scented himself every day with one of the very first lavender-scented eau de Colognes, created by Jean-Marie Farina, thus adding to its triumphant success.

Happy almost anywhere

In recent times lavender has gradually ceased to be a wild shrub and has crept into the domestic garden. A few lavender bushes can transform a small plot of earth in Italy, Spain or even in England into a colourful, scented Provençal paradise. English gardeners have crossbred, multiplied and improved – as is the correct term – the plant so that some varieties can resist the northern winter, while others bear exceptionally large blooms.

Today, lavender is cultivated throughout the world. It is grown to produce essential oil in Provence, in Piedmont in Italy, in Spain, in

Children selling bunches of fresh lavender at the turn of the twentieth century on the streets of London.

Bulgaria, in the Crimea and even, just recently, in China. Throughout Europe, as well as in the USA, Australia and Japan, it is planted in gardens, where it is appreciated for its beauty and its fragrant scent.

Yet in spite of all of this popularity, the best perfume makers use only Provençal lavender. In an industry of fragrances and cosmetics almost entirely dominated by synthetic smells, the natural fragrance of lavender is synonymous with authenticity and natural well-being. Closely associated with both our health and our beauty, lavender is as

·LAVENDER'S · BLVE ·

La - ven - der's   blue, did-dle, did-dle! La - ven - der's   green;

When I   am   king, diddle. diddle!   You shall be   queen.

2. Call up your men, diddle, diddle!
   Set them to work;
   Some to the plough, diddle, diddle!
   Some to the cart.

3. Some to make hay, diddle, diddle!
   Some to cut corn;
   While you and I, diddle, diddle!
   Keep ourselves warm.

Left: Score of "Lavender's Blue" from Walter Crane's *The Baby Opera*, 1845. In those days Lavender played an important role in Anglo-Saxon culture.

Right: An eau de Cologne advert from the turn of the twentieth century; many eau de Colognes were lavender-scented at that time.

Below: Lavender water made in Provence was sold locally in small plain bottles.

much used in the daily treatment of small injuries as it is for gaining a good night's sleep.

More recently, lavender has brought an original touch to experimental and inventive cookery. Gourmets, good cooks and famous chefs all use the scented calyxes in their recipes and some French restaurants even offer entire lavender-based menus. It adds a subtle note to sweet and savoury dishes, a fresh, sunny, herbal and floral flavour. Iced melon soup with olive oil and lavender, caramelized lavender flowers or lavender and peach jam invite every food lover to sample the flavour of tranquil summers spent lying in the shade of a tree listening to the chant of the cicadas.

Lavender pleases all the senses. A handful of dried stems or a few petals create a decorative, scented ambience that can fill the home, while plaited dollies and embroidered linen sachets filled with dried flowers scent drawers and wardrobes, repelling undesirable insects.

In Provence and elsewhere, this enchanting plant encountered on pastoral walks and summer nights offers a link with nature whether it is used in the home, in the garden, as a fragrance or as a culinary seasoning.

In lavender country

The blue gold of Provence

For many years, lavender was only thought of as a wild plant, practically a weed that belonged in the countryside, a plant of no particular interest. It rarely appeared in written documents before the end of the nineteenth century, and although doctors and naturalists had been familiar with the plant for hundreds of years, its 'civilized' life in France only began after the 1870s.

At the end of the nineteenth century, self-seeding Provençal mountain lavender only grew above 800 metres and covered the mountains of Upper Provence and Lower Dauphiné. In those days, the cultivation of nutritious cereal crops like rye and spelt was considered essential. The local authorities only permitted wild lavender flowers to be cut and gathered once the harvest was over.

Lavender flowers were picked on all the mountain slopes of Provence and on those found as far north as the Diois, and in the foothills of the Vercors. Lucienne Roubin, the author of *Monde des odeurs* (*The world of scents*), a passionate study of life in a small village in the 1880s around the time when wild lavender was collected, tells of how everyone took part: "When the cutting begins, everyone, apart from young mothers and the elderly, goes to collect flowers. Perfume makers from Grasse make purchasing agreements with some of the villagers to buy the cut lavender and bring it right to Grasse… The villages are at that time awash with the balsamic fragrance of the flowers. For, every summer, the inhabitants of the mountain gather several dozen tons of lavender on the rocky slopes of their land."

Young pickers sold their crops to chemists in Lyon, notably to the Gattefossé family. These chemists were the first to begin cultivating

lavender and develop an interest in the quality of the various distillations and in the therapeutic use of essential oils.

Lavender and sheep

At the end of the nineteenth century, on the hillsides of Provence and the southern Pre-Alps, farmers divided their time between two main activities: raising sheep and picking lavender. The sheep kept the weeds down on the land naturally. They fertilized the soil and grazed on plants that would otherwise have restricted the growth of the small lavender clumps. Beyond that, farmers only needed to keep their flocks away from the young shoots in spring, and to wait for the plants to flower, ready for picking. Trees didn't grow back on mountains that were overrun by sheep, creating ideal conditions for growing lavender, which benefits from full sun and does not do well in competition with abundant vegetation.

Country people picked lavender at an altitude of around 1,000 metres after 14 July, when the tiny flowers on the tips of the spikes start to

Above: Sheep don't eat lavender stems. They keep the weeds down in areas where lavender grows naturally by feeding off other vegetation.

Right: In summer, around the turn of the twentieth century, the whole family took part in cutting lavender on the high-altitude *baïassières*. (From the collection of Bernard Laget)

drop. Work was organized using the only available workforce, the family. A lavender shrub was tackled using a 'reverse' manoeuvre, which means using a backward facing palm to grab a bunch of stems with one hand before cutting them with a sickle held in the other. Flowers and stems were then placed in the apron or a large sack. Once this was full, it was tipped into a *bourras*, a large piece of coarsely woven canvas made of hemp or cotton and linen, that was knotted in all four corners to make it easier to carry the contents.

When the picking area was located near the village, families spent all day gathering lavender and returned to their farms at nightfall. But if their homesteads were far away, they would live on the mountain for the duration, sleeping under the stars with their heads in the shelter of a box tree, using their *bourras* as a sleeping bag.

An ass or mule was used to carry a small portable still that could be easily dismantled. During picking time, the older pickers would look for a spring or a stream source that would provide the necessary water for distillation, while the children found wood for heating. The small still was set up on several flat stones and entrusted to the oldest member of the family, less capable of running round the mountain.

The first documentary evidence that mentions ownership of a domestic still is an eighteenth-century marriage contract from the Forcalquier area, listing goods belonging to the wife. It may have been one of those small copper models known as *tête-de-Maure* (moor's head). These were only ever used to distil lavender and can still be seen at the Musée de la Lavande at Coustellet in the Vaucluse.

Local village blacksmiths produced the stills, and their shapes, which were often irregular, varied according to the expertise of the craftsman and his skill in hammering copper.

The round container was filled with around 100 kilograms of cut flowers mixed with water. The lid, a conical-shaped hat or top, was soldered with a clay coil and topped by a swan's neck joined onto a condenser, a coil that concentrated the perfumed vapour. A fire was lit just under the bowl, between the stones that held it in place. The intensity of the heat, and therefore the length of the distillation process, depended on the oils contained in the different woods that were used (pine, evergreen oak, juniper etc.) and on the diameter of the logs.

The birth of an industry

Wagon teams belonging to the lavender brokers, representatives of the perfume makers from Grasse, travelled back and forth across the

Edition A. Mounier

2 7bre 1921

Distillerie DUSSERRE, Gap
Specialité : *Lavande, Bouquet des Alpes*
Nouvelle création : *Fleur de nos Montagnes*

Above: A still carried on a wagon drawn by a mule in Hautes-Alpes at the beginning of the twentieth century. (From the collection of Bernard Laget)

Left: Distilling in the middle of wild lavender fields, using small individual copper stills, known as *têtes-de-maure* (Moor's head). (From the collection of Bernard Laget)

Right: In the area around Grasse, eau de toilettes made with a lavender essence base were kept in small porcelain flasks. (Musée des Arômes, Saint-Rémy-de-Provence)

Antique stills at the Musée de Coustellet, in the Lubéron

Far left: A large copper still with a superb condensation coil for cooling.

Left: A small mobile still

Right: Each still proudly wears the manufacturers' label and the prices paid during the years it operated.

Below: Lavender essential oil was collected in *essenciers* made of tin or containers made of zinc or copper.

mountains from the first days of summer, loading up with the crops of flowering stems before distillation. From the beginning of the twentieth century, the wagons were replaced by lorries, in order to get around to all the small places in a more efficient manner. On these, people from the distilleries officiated and weighed the crops. During the first half of the summer, the mountain buzzed like a hive. Lavender pickers ran all over the place; the most efficient could collect nearly 100 kilograms of flowers in just a day. Competition for the best collections was tough among the perfume companies' representatives.

In 1910, a German company called Schimmel built the first distillery that was not owned by the Grasse perfume factories, right in the centre of the collecting area at Barrême, in the Alpes-de-Haute-Provence, and soon after they built a second on the Sault plateau in the Vaucluse. Some of the mountain folk, meanwhile, continued to distil what they themselves had collected, using artisan stills that had slowly increased in size until they could process over 150 kilograms of flowers in the body of the still. The lavender industry was born, and with it recognition of the value and quality of the essential oil of lavender grown in Provence.

Brokers began to return later in summer, once the distillation was over, not to buy lavender flowers, but the distilled essential oils. A new form of knowledge developed: brokers had to learn where the best wild lavender grew – 'the best *baïassières*' as they are called by the people of

20

Provence, *baïasse* being a clump or cluster of lavender. Essential oil buyers learned to differentiate the distillations, the good vintages from the less refined, and to recognize the fragrance of essences derived from flowers grown on south-facing slopes that get more sun (and are finer), from those of flowers grown on north-facing slopes.

The container or can of essential oil made of tin was inscribed with the name of the producer and the place where the oil was made. Lavender essences from different sources that are blended together are called an *assemblage* – a term also used in wine-making – and are known by the places of origin.

Coming down from the mountain…

From the beginning of the twentieth century, lavender cutting yielded a healthy profit. There was even a saying: "Good ground for lavender clusters is worth more than a field of wheat!" But gathering lavender on

steep stony slopes was demanding work. Men and even children had to work extremely hard for long hours to fill and then carry the *bourras*, weighing between 60 and 80 kilograms each, to where the cart could take over. It might have been possible to carry a spade for hoeing the earth to remove weeds but any real digging was out of the question on the side of the mountain.

That is why, from the beginning of the twentieth century, lavender started to come down from the high mountain slopes to be cultivated in regularly spaced rows in fields closer to villages. Pioneering growers attempted to transplant wild plants at lower altitudes, to sow them… and they succeeded!

Slowly, lavender cultivation progressed to the detriment of the old method of gathering. In the mid-twentieth century the Provençal landscape was changing; only areas with heavy clay soils escaped – these were kept for livestock farming. This was the 'totally blue' period in Provence. However, although the harvesting increased the tonnage, it also revealed the delicate nature of the flowers that have to be quickly taken to the still for immediate processing. If this brief time span is extended in any way, it places the grower's profit at stake!

To cope with the increased crop of flowers, distillation processes also evolved. Stills grew larger and became fixed installations sheltered in huge barns. A new steam distillation technique was developed whereby the flowers were no longer soaked in water, and dry lavender straw was conserved and could then be reused as fuel.

From the 1970s, mechanical harvesting made cultivation on small plots of land and steep slopes even more difficult. Plateaus at a height of

Above left: Women gathering lavender in England in the 1950s (On Seal Farm near Sevenoaks, Kent)

Right: Blue-flowering spikes of true lavender, chosen for its colour.

between 700 and 1,000 metres, such as Sault and Valensole, were covered in vast rows of lavender. The landscape changed. Up above, wild mountain lavender was gradually left alone – men climbed up the steep slopes less often and the plants were neglected by sheep, too. Broom, small bushes, then pine trees began to grow in the abandoned areas, forcing the wild sun-loving lavender to retreat. The high Provençal prairies that were once covered throughout the year in various successive shades of blue slowly became green.

'Grosse' lavender

In Provence people still remember that *grosse* (large) lavender, the hybrids that appear naturally by cross-pollination of true mountain lavender with the spike lavender of the plains, was always found at intermediate altitudes, where the two varieties grew side by side. Its bushes grow more vigorously than those of fine or medicinal lavender but its essential oil, which is less refined, was held to be of little value by the perfume industry. No one bothered to collect the flowers. And that's how it remained until the invention of the washing machine in the United States of America.

In fact, during the 1930s, washing powder manufacturers were trying to find a means of deodorizing the unpleasant smell of powders that were beginning to replace the soap used by the laundress. The distilleries and perfume makers at Grasse were asked to come up with a solution, and the essential oils of both fine and spike lavender were shown to be suitable. But the small yields of these two varieties could never have satisfied the American market. A broker from Montbrun-les-Bains, to the south of the Mont Ventoux – an ancestor of the Reynaud family, which is still a leading producer of lavender essential oil – decided to try distilling the flowers of 'grosse' lavender. And so lavandin was born, with the promise of a great international future in the manufacture of washing powder.

This variety produces an excellent yield and also grows on low altitude ground. Cultivation took off rapidly from the 1950s. Today lavandin – often mistakenly called lavender – grows in most areas of Provence. Its flowers colour the plains and the limestone plateaus with deep violet shades, and make the summer sky seem pale by comparison with its strong blues. It surrounds old stone farmhouses with great fields of colour during the first days of July and in winter presents endless grey rows of plants that offer a striking contrast with the russet colour of the oak trees under which truffles grow.

Parallel rows in an arc-shaped lavandin field at the height of their flowering season in the first days of July.

24

Lavender landscapes

Recently, lavender cultivation has completely altered the plant's geographic territory: the blue mountain flowers now grow on the lower altitude plains and plateaus of a Provence that is more accessible and more familiar to tourists. In the Alpes-de-Haute-Provence, lavandin covers the Valensole plateau, stretching out to the foot of the Montagne de Lure and around Banon and Simiane-la-Rotonde. In the Drôme area, it flowers on the hills and plateaus of the Pre-Alps, between Dieulefit, Grignan and Nyons, and in the Baronnies area. Fine lavender (*L. angustifolia*) still remains at higher altitudes, flourishing on the Sault plateau and on high ground at Ferrassières and Mévouillon.

Glorious lavandins

The lavender season begins with the summer solstice and lasts until the beginning of August, for late-flowering mountain plants. From the middle of June the first lavish tufts of lavandin start to colour the plains. In the beginning, there is only a hint of greenish blue, shimmering like a discreet halo that disappears in strong light. The shade starts to deepen rapidly and, in less than three weeks, has reached its finest hue, a dense, saturated violet of an astonishing visual intensity. Then the colour fades, the lavandin turning purplish mauve and gradually greying. At this stage, which is generally around mid-July, the flowering stems are ready for cutting.

The last days of June and the first days of July – though the uncertainties of the weather can bring this forward or set it back by a week – are therefore the ideal time for being amid the lavender, exploring the paths and byways of the region. Alongside the wheat, the

grape vines, sunflowers and flowering broom bushes, the various lavender varieties create a bright, lively palette of contrasting colours that could have belonged to an artist such as Van Gogh or Matisse.

From the Roche-Saint-Secret to the Montagne de Lure

In the Roche-Saint-Secret Valley, not far from Dieulefit, a sea of lavender extends over both sides of the valley, catching the light of the passing day. Perched high up and tumbling down the steep slopes, some plantations accentuate the contours of the land, while others gently circle the mountain. The rows of lavender are regularly spaced or grouped in threes between rows of young truffle oaks. From a distance they appear to blend together, covering the earth, like a vast blue blanket. On days when the Mistral blows, a heavy swell rises in the lavender fields and the plant stems sway in waves like the surface of a stormy sea, revealing a kaleidoscope of metallic greens and blues.

The stony ground is visible between the lavender clusters where no other plants can grow, except for perhaps a few grasses whose delicate airy inflorescences are lovely to see. Sometimes a few apricots ripen on the trees just as the lavender flowers, hinting at unusual and innovative culinary possibilities.

Farther south, Tricastin's vine stocks and the Enclave des Papes' truffle fields run alongside the small fields of lavender. This is the home of

Above: Cultivated lavandin alternating with young oak trees in a truffle plantation near Grignan.

Right: Lavandin and wheat planted side by side on the Valensole plateau, in the Alpes-de-Haute-Provence.

Below: Lavandins and olive trees form a harmonious ensemble of blues and silvers.

great stone Provençal farmhouses that are sometimes fortified, of old ruined villages set high up in the mountains and abandoned in the nineteenth century for settlements at the bottom of the hills and of medieval towers and châteaux. From time to time, thick plumes of smoke from a distillery built right in the centre of the village rise up and scent the surrounding countryside.

At sunset, the hilltop village of Grignan, surrounded by lavender fields and overlooked by a collegiate church and a château haunted by memories of the famous literary Madame de Sévigné, is bathed in a flattering pink light that comes from the flowering lavender bushes. All around, lavender and truffle fields form a harmonious landscape, a

Grignan, whose château was made famous by the writer Madame de Sévigné, is a hilltop village, perched like an island in the middle of fields of lavandin.

wonderful sight in any season. A few rows of lavender are planted between the rows of young oak trees during the first ten years, before they begin to produce truffles. This gives a small harvest and some return during the truffle field's non-productive years. It also favours the growth of the black truffles, as lavender's deep roots aerate the soil and help to prepare it. After about ten years, when the old clusters of lavandin begin to wither, the truffle field comes into production. In some places, old shrivelled lavandin plants still bring forth a few blue flowers in the summer, and in winter they often shelter the best truffles. Still farther south, and a little later in mid-July, lavandin flowers at the foot of the Montagne de Lure, around villages built high up in the

Left: The Romanesque church, walled cemetery and presbytery at Solérieux, a tiny village in the Provençal Drôme, stands over a blue scented swathe of lavender.

Right: On the Sault plateau, in the north of the Vaucluse, many *bories*, typical old stone shelters, are dotted among the fields growing lavender *angustifolia*.

Overleaf: Near Ferrassières, between the Mont Ventoux and the Lubéron, the *angustifolia* lavenders with their differing blue, mauve, purple and sometimes pink shades stretch as far as the eye can see. In the background a plot of land glows a uniform deep blue. Here the shrubs whose flowers were too pale in colour have been removed.

mountains. Simiane-la-Rotonde, a village overlooked by a twelfth-century rotunda of unknown origins, sits in the middle of cultivated scented plants. On the way up to the village, a wave of violet lavandin breaks just as the clary sage finishes flowering, showing just a hint of pale pink.

Banon, a few kilometres farther on, is an old fortified town famous for a fine goats' cheese wrapped in chestnut leaves. It too is surrounded by stretches of lavender. On the plateau above the village the sight of hundred-year-old chestnut trees alongside lavender fields is quite surprising. Generally, these trees need a damp climate and don't grow on the chalky, arid soils preferred by lavender. This is a curious exception to the botanical rule, and an explanation has never been found, but it is one of summer's spectacular and almost magical sights.

The herbalists' mountain

At the beginning of August on the top of the Montagne de Lure – the herbalists' mountain – true lavender (*L. angustifolia*) is gathered in the same way as it used to be over a century ago. The picking-grounds are reached by climbing up through the village of Redortiers and past the Contadour hamlet, made famous by the twentieth-century French novelist Jean Giono. From there, on foot, the route continues towards the Jas des terres du Roux sheep pens, crossing the *baïassières* (an old Provençal term for the places where the lavender clumps grow) colonized by yellow-flowering St John's-wort and gentian-blue hyssop.

This is a landscape dominated by dovecotes, substantial towers roofed in terracotta tiles.

Up on the Sault plateau wild lavender is already in flower by the second week of July. It lasts for a whole month, sometimes longer. Depending on the light, the Mont Ventoux on the horizon can appear quite close but at other times it seems far away. Here, every piece of ground that is not covered in cereal crops is lavender-blue. The blue varies, changing colour depending on whether the lavender fields are seen close up or from far away. Sometimes the blue can be a shade of mauve, turning grey or violet, and sometimes a pale blue that is almost white, or a deep violet colour, almost purple.

Nuances of colour gently vibrate through the seas of lavender, softening the rhythm of evenly spaced rows of the fields. They derive from plantings of stocks sown from seed, which means that each shrub differs slightly from its neighbour: the stems can be long or short, the number of flowers on the spikes is highly variable and the flowering times are staggered. Pink lavender is the last to flower, and its spikes will still be grey in the middle of a field dominated by mauve and violet flowers.

Some of the most beautiful lavender plantations in Provence are situated around Ferrassières and the Château de la Gabelle, where Marguerite Blanc and her family have been cultivating acres of various types of lavender for generations. These perfectly composed blue expanses seem to be patched with occasional small squares of intense violet – this is the lavender used for making bouquets. The back of the valley is covered in swathes of bushes that are still green and barely clouded with a blue haze. This is lavandin, which is picked only for its flowers, used to fill small scented sachets.

In the heat of high summer, the slightest noise sends red-winged grasshoppers leaping. The flowers hum with the buzzing of determined bees – walkers, pickers cutting and gathering, nothing seems to scare them away. So when the time comes to cut off the lavender flowers with a small sickle, leaving behind round green plant cushions, every cutter's arms are covered in insect bites and stings by the end of the day.

Despite this, each year at the beginning of August, 40,000 bouquets of lavender are cut by hand to keep their stems intact, and hung upside down to dry. Each bouquet weighs around 60 grams and, for a whole year, they will retain their beautiful violet colour, which is produced by the calyxes of the flower; the petals fall out as the bouquets dry.

Right: Cultivated for making bouquets, 'Super-blue' is still cut with a small hand-sickle. Grown from carefully selected cuttings, it is a deeper shade of blue than other lavenders and bears longer stems.

Overleaf: Once they have been made from fresh flowers, bouquets are hung upside down to dry for two months in dark, well-ventilated storage room.

Below: At the beginning of August, harvesting Lavandula *angustifolia* 'Super-blue' progressively strips the rows in the lavender fields.

Every family treasures its own secrets about their choice of lavender varieties here. For each of them, the knowledge is a personal wealth that has been patiently acquired through experience and observation, in a practical manner, over many generations.

At the Château de la Gabelle, only the roots of intensely coloured flowers with long stems are kept to provide the mother plant for the nursery and thus, provide the plants for 'Super-blue' lavender.

Other plots of lavender are mechanically harvested, without special care, and dried on the ground before being put in the crusher to separate the flowers and stems. The stems are used as bedding in the sheep pens. They are said to have prophylactic powers so their use guarantees healthy ewes in the last links of a perfect ecological chain: after picking, the sheep are put out to pasture on the lavender fields, assuring a system of fertilization as natural as it is efficient.

Hence, Marguerite Blanc's plantations have a long history: "Today we speak of sustainable agriculture," remarks this indefatigable woman, smiling, "but it is actually just a question of doing what our ancestors did."

The cradle of 'Super-blue'

Today, the Mévouillon Valley, in the Baronnies, where cereal crops were grown in the past, is a huge prairie and one has to look up to catch sight of the plants for which it is famous, growing on the sunny slopes above: the lavender and lavandin bushes that grow alongside other aromatic plants… This is where the first selections of blue lavender, which is grown for its flowers, and of 'Super-blue' lavender for making bouquets, are made.

Between the hamlet of Gresse and the 'fort' at Mévouillon – the name of an astonishing rock formation – the hill slopes carry small patches of colourful, intense violet-blue fields, sometimes only tiny in size. Lower down on the projecting shelf, spelt ripens, an ancient small-eared cereal crop that turns the fields a pale golden-blond.

At the end of summer, mountains of lavender straw grow around drying areas created as soon as the harvesting of cereals is over. These are left over from stripping the lavender and will be composted before being used to fertilize the fields from whence they came.

As for the flowers of 'Super-blue', they will have been made into bouquets and then hung up to dry in drying rooms.

Kitchen gardens and a lavender nursery with tight rows of young plants are planted beside the path leading to the fort.

Right: Spikes varying in length, staggered flowering times, intense, variable colours: a field of true lavender sown from seed.

Below: Marguerite Blanc makes gorgeous traditional bouquets by adding stems round and round and then finishing off with a crown of ears of wheat.

Above: Lavender being farmed in Australia, along the Great Ocean Road. In the second half of the twentieth century, lavender, hitherto confined to Mediterranean soil, gradually began to extend to other horizons.

Left: Farmed lavender in the hills of the Provençale Drôme. Their uniformity of colour is achieved by reproducing plants from cuttings from a single selected plant.

Right at the back of this little valley, behind an old orchard, lavender grows in a pastoral landscape where it isn't hard to envision a shepherd with a herd of goats, his ewes with their bells, the braying of an ass tied to a tree, the watchful gaze of the dog looking after the animals… Here lavender is still picked as it was in the nineteenth century, by hand. Walnut and young lime trees, as well as the small stone walls that border tiny patches of land prohibit the passage of agricultural machinery. The lime trees growing on the road verges are pruned and shaped and offer a striking contrast to the walnut trees, which are left to develop naturally. The limes are trained into balls to be as high as they are wide to facilitate the collection of the flowers – Baronnies linden blossom is very famous, and beehives that are placed here produce delicious lime honey.

Just a few feet away, the Mont Ventoux rises up towering above a small lavender distillery, which perfumes the countryside during August.

Winter greys

If summer is a season filled with colours and textures, then winter is the season for rhythm and structure. The earth is never bare here. Devoid

of their colourful flowers and lavish growth, the lavender fields are naturally less spectacular but now resemble grey-green tapestries. Their straight rows neatly structure an easily discernible landscape or form an endless series of lines running off to the horizon. Sometimes the successive waves of perfect geometry that comb the landscape struggle with the natural undulations of the ground and form a series of curves to take account of an awkward or irregular plot, creating sophisticated graphic designs.

The beginning of winter, when the locals take their dogs to hunt for truffles, is a wonderful time for long walks. The oak trees have turned russet, the olive trees are laden with fruit about to be gathered, the rows of lavender are silvery grey, the sky is clear blue, everything is in perfect harmony!

At the beginning of spring when the almond trees blossom, the lavender plants are still in the grip of winter, waiting until April or May before discreetly putting forth fresh green shoots with touches of ash, at a time when nature presents its most exuberant greens.

Above: Even during the grey winter season, the rows of lavender sculpture the landscape.

Right: Rows of lavender interspersed with oak trees on a truffle farm receive the visits of the truffle hunters until the middle of winter.

Previous pages: True lavender is a hardy species. Every winter, snow covers the Sault plateau with a thick blanket of snow creating an isolated landscape of mysterious reflections.

The scented soul of lavender

"In the solitude of the Montagne de Lure [...] at picking time, the scent of lavender hangs in the evening air. The sunset's rays fall on wagons loaded with cut flowers. Rudimentary stills established near water cisterns blow red flames into the night air. The caramel-scented smoke from their flames is carried on the wind and enchants the sleep of those that sleep alone in the wilderness." This short piece of writing by Jean Giono, published in the magazine *La France et ses parfums* (*Fragrances of France*) in 1958, paints an image of lavender distillation in the middle of the twentieth century.

Since then, most of these installations have become industrialized. However, they still operate on the same principle – the distillation of lavender flowers extracts their essence or perfume and captures their quintessential soul.

When the harvest starts, endless lines of lorries come and go to feed the large industrial distilleries, while tractors loaded with dried sheaves supply the small traditional installations. The first sign of chimney smoke signals the start of an intensive period of hard work but at the same time provokes a sigh of relief – at last the value of the harvest will be known!

The harvest

The short picking period lasts from the beginning of July to the middle of August, depending on whether lavender or lavandin is being gathered, and on the plantation's altitude. When over half the flowers are still closed on the spike, the yield of essential oil is at its highest. This is when the cutter starts, leaving bundles of flowering stems alongside rows of green plants cut short. To evaporate some of the water

49

contained in the plant, the cut sheaves are left on top of the trimmed lavender clumps to dry for three or four days before loading them onto trucks that will take them to the distillery. As they wilt, the flowers turn mauve, greying after a few hours, which creates a new spectacle: one of green garlands punctuated by mauve bouquets alongside the last violet rows waiting to be cut. The traditional method of cutting and drying sheaves on the field is, however, gradually disappearing, threatened by the crushed-plant method of harvesting, which is becoming more widely used.

Harvest is the most hazardous time of the year, when even the threat of a simple summer storm is a constant source of worry for all lavender growers. Rain can be catastrophic for a plant that is ready for picking but has not yet been cut. The flowers can turn mouldy, making the batch of extracted essences unusable by tainting them with nasty odours. In order to cultivate lavender, more than many other plants, it is therefore necessary to keep a close eye on another great shade of blue, that of the sky above.

When distillation scents the air...

Fumes from the Pré du Jas distillery scent the air in the small village of Villeperdrix, located above the Eygues gorges, in the Nyons Pre-Alps. The still's small fire, initially lit with a few old logs, is supplemented with lavender straw that has just come out of the vat.

Everything here is done just as it was in the old days: the distiller, Bernard Ducros, gets the still going in a manner not dissimilar to scalding a tea pot... He passes steam through to clean the conduits and to warm them. Then he empties fine lavender that has been brought tied up in great canvas cloths into the main tank and tramples it down to pack it in. The fire is relit, the container is sealed and distillation begins: a mixture of water, fire and plants. Fairly quickly, water that at first is just slightly oily starts to flow into the *essencier*, the container where the oil is collected. It becomes gradually oilier and finally, towards the end of the process, quite clear and light in colour. After about 45 minutes the 200 kilograms of fine lavender (*angustifolia*) packed into the main receptacle of the still will have yielded less than two litres of golden, scented essential oil. It is organic oil, as this small still is only used for distilling plants grown without pesticides or wild lavender grown at altitude that is naturally 'organic'.

In Nyons, on the banks of the river Eygues, another distillery scents the air of the small town all summer long. It has an evocative name,

Above: In summer, the Nyons distillery perfumes the entire town. Earlier in the season, thyme and other aromatic plants are distilled here.

Previous pages: At the beginning of August, Bernard Ducros, picker and distiller, harvests wild lavender at 1,200 metres altitude amid the rocky landscape of the Montagne d'Angèle.

Bleu Provence, but its installation comprises of a sheet metal roof, a tall chimney for evacuating the smoke and the traditional lavender straw-fuelled boiler with a tangle of pipes. The scent of the distilled lavender impregnates clothing – a heavy, heady smell when it is lavandin, but an intoxicating and euphoric fragrance where true lavender is concerned.

The three large containers at the Nyons distillery each have to be filled in turn with 300 kilograms of flowers. Four apprentices work in relays from dawn to dusk. They pack the lavender into the containers and close them, feeding the fire with the straw still steaming from the previous distillation and waiting for the essential oil to float to the top

of the oil-and-water mixture before drawing it off. Once a distillation is done, they unlock the lid of the still and lift out the inside basket that usually contains several hundred kilograms of lavender bundles that have been distilled. White steam, full of heady perfume, fills the distillery. But there is no question of slacking, as the containers need to be refilled immediately for another run.

It is hard work, but there are a few intervals when gardeners from the surrounding areas, realizing from the scent of perfume pervading the village that the still is in operation, deliver their own modest lavandin harvests. One of the apprentices carefully weighs and notes each delivery so that half of the essence produced from it can be returned to the amateur grower while the other is kept by the distiller in payment for his work.

Distilling lavender is neither taught at school nor learned from a book. The ancient technique is only passed on from master to apprentice through shared experience of the work. Often, a father teaches his son the secrets of distillation and sometimes a distiller, wanting to hand down his passion, imparts his knowledge to one of his aides. Many of the distillers, who today produce extremely high-quality essential oils for aromatherapy, started out picking wild plants. They brought with them a good botanical knowledge of the local flora and were then able to find their own formulae in the distillation process.

Above: Work at the Pré du Jas distillery continues as it did over a hundred years ago, overlooking the mountains of the Baronnies area. Lavender arrives tied in *bourras* piled high on wagons. They are trampled down to pack them into the still's single main container. Lavender straw and old stocks burn in the entrance.

Overleaf: Steam rising from lavender straw after the distillation fills the country-side. Once dried, the straw will be burned to fuel future distillations.

Of fire and water

Distillation is a mechanical process for extracting essential oils from a scented plant. At the end of the process, the essence – or essential oil (the two are synonymous) – that is obtained is the same as that which is naturally produced by the plant but it has the advantage of being immediately available, extremely concentrated and easy to transport and store.

Pressurized water vapour is injected into a sealed tank that resembles a huge kind of pressure-cooker, filled with flowers or sheaves of lavender. The heat and the pressure meet and fracture the walls of the small cells in the lavender that contain the essence, vaporizing it. The essential oil molecules are drawn out of the tank into the swan's neck of the still in the form of vapour. The mixture of water vapour and essential oil is then cooled as it travels through a condenser – a long, coiled copper pipe that passes through cold water – and empties into the *essencier* or collecting vessel. Once there, the oil and water separate naturally on account of the different densities of the two liquids: the essence, which is lighter than water, floats on top and is easily collected. The distillation water, called the hydrolat or floral water, holds a small percentage of residual essence as well as the active water-soluble constituents of the plant.

In the distillery, essential oil is measured by weight rather than by volume. The quantity of oil that a plant contains is extremely variable: 50 kilograms of lavandin flowers yield one kilogram of essential oil. It

Above: The new crushing method of harvesting lavender is responsible for the disappearance of wagons loaded with sweet smelling sheaves in the countryside.

Left: Towards the end of the distillation process, the mixture of water and essential oil runs out of the condenser into the essencier, where they are decanted.

takes twice as much fine lavender to obtain the same amount of oil. By comparison, to obtain just one kilogram of rose essential oil about four tons of flowers are required.

Recently a new mechanized process has been imported from the USA. This 'crushed-plant process' is mainly used for distilling lavandin. Most distilleries have rapidly adapted to its use.

Lavender flowers and stems are cut and crushed by a machine and ejected through a pipe into a container. When it is full, this is taken to the distillery, tightly sealed and connected to incoming pressurized vapour on one side and to an evacuation system for the vapour carrying the essential oil on the other. The whole operation is as rapid as a combine harvester, depriving lavender lovers, however, of the colourful sight of the harvesting and transportation of sheaves to the distillery.

In economic terms, mechanical harvesting of this kind offers considerable savings compared to harvesting by hand, both in the lavender field and at the distillery, but purists are critical of the new distillation techniques. They judge the quality of the essences obtained to be barely satisfactory and their conservation period uncertain. In France today, this procedure is still only used for producing lavandin essences for use in the washing industry. Fine lavender is still distilled in the traditional way.

Lavender in the garden

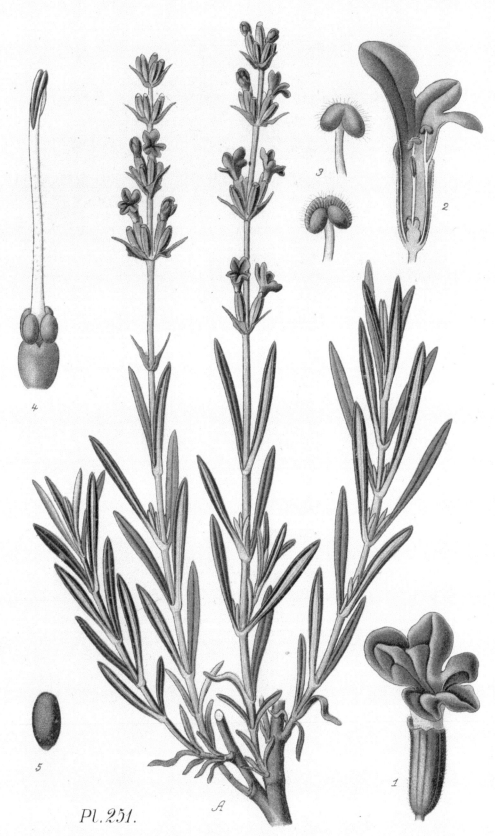

Pl. 251.

Lavande officinale. Lavandula officinalis L.

A touch of botany

Previous pages: Blue and
white lavandin set off by
rugged purple verbena
in the Filippi nursery's
lavender garden.

Left: *Lavendula angustifolia*,
botanical illustration from
a late-nineteenth-century
book of herbs.

Below: *Lavandula stoechas*
in flower.

Lavender, or rather lavenders, are naturally native to dry, sunny countries. Their habitat begins in Provence, and extends south, all around the Mediterranean.

But human passion can create heroic feats: in past centuries, botanists and gardeners have discovered how to make this plant flourish in countries where the climate is not really suited to it, and so today England is the true cradle of garden lavender.

Around the Mediterranean

Like many scented plants, lavender belongs to the *Labiatae* or mint family, together with thyme, rosemary, hyssop, savory and many other aromatic plants. Only three species of lavender exist in the wild, in the south of France, Italy or Spain: *Lavandula latifolia* or spike lavender; *Lavandula angustifolia* or true lavender, also called fine, medicinal and English lavender; and *Lavandula stœchas*, also known as French lavender.

Spike lavender grows on stony chalk-based soils at altitudes below 600 metres. Its flowers are at their best in late summer. The tightly packed bracts on a central spike contain tiny flowers, light mauve or pale blue, with grey calyxes. The leaves are large, grey and scented, and the fairly small clumps smell strongly camphorous. This rarely cultivated lavender is usually picked wild and distilled for its essence, which is used in aromatherapy. In the past it was used as an ingredient in oil paints and in the days when paints were made in the studio, artists like Titian and Veronese used lavender oil. In fact, its presence or absence in pigment analysis is a means of dating a painting.

True lavender grows in full sunlight on well drained ground and on limestone outcrops 700 metres above sea level, clambering up the slopes of Mediterranean mountains as high as 1,400 metres. Its preferred home is Provence in France, but it also grows in northern Spain and Piedmont in Italy. The woody stock roots firmly in the soil and produces a low clump bearing narrow, linear grey leaves. It comes into flower in mid-range altitudes towards the end of June, but at altitudes above 1,200 metres this is pushed back to the beginning of August. The inflorescence takes the form of short spikes bearing rings of dozens of tiny flowers that in themselves are minuscule. They only have a single corolla whose upper lip is drawn back. Their colour varies from pale blue, through mauve to violet. The plant's precious substance, its essential oil, is mostly contained in the calyx, in cells entirely protected by microscopic hairs. This is what enables the plant to lie for a few days after cutting without this in any way affecting or altering its essence.

Where spike lavender ends and true lavender begins, the two species interbreed, due to cross-pollination by bees, producing *L.* x *intermedia*. Known as lavandin, these hybrid plants grow vigorously and bear many of the characteristics of their parent plants. However, their essential oil is less refined and always more camphorous. It took a long time to realize that the plants were sterile hybrids that do not produce seeds and therefore need to be reproduced from cuttings.

L. stœchas, French, tufted, Moorish or butterfly lavender, is the only variety that grows well in acid soil. It grows in France in the Maures and Estérel mountains and on islands of the Levant (also known as the Hyères), but is also found in north-eastern Spain, Greece and Turkey. It flowers once at the end of winter and again in autumn, producing square purple spikes topped with small violet leaves that look like two little wings. It gets its name of 'papillon' or butterfly lavender from these leaves, and there are other grey leaves all along its short stem.

Today botanists have listed more than 30 varieties of lavender. Many of them naturally cross-breed all around the Mediterranean, including the Balearic Islands, Cyprus and Crete. Some have spread as far as Ethiopia, Somalia and the Yemen, while others have taken root in Atlantic islands like the Azores, Madeira, the Canaries and as far as the subtropical climate of the Cape Verde Islands.

In Spain, apart from the naturally occurring spike and true lavender in the north-east and the lavandin cultivated on the high arid plains of

Right: *Lavandula lanata*, a Spanish species with ash-white woolly leaves.

Below: *Lavandula spica*, illustration by M. Hérincq, 1906.

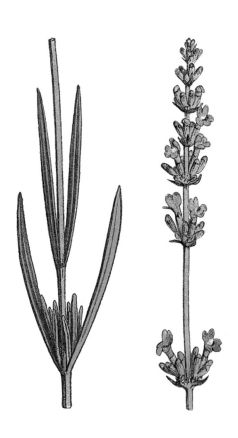

Valladolid north of Madrid, there are three wonderful wild species that grow naturally in the south of the country: *L. lanata* (woolly lavender), *L. dentata* (another French lavender) and *L. multifida* (French lace lavender). *L. lanata* forms a low cushion of ash-white, woolly leaves. It produces dark violet spikes at the end of summer. The leaves of *L. dentata* are light green, with finely serrated edges and the plant produces light blue flowers that last for most of the year. *L. multifida*, with highly aromatic, finely indented leaves, presents violet-blue flowers from March to November.

Two species of wild lavender grow in Madeira and the Canary Islands, *L. pinnata* (Spanish mountain lavender) and *L. minutolii*. *L. pinnata* has silver-grey lobed leaves and *L. minutolii* has feather-like leaves. Although such plants come originally from gentle climates and in their natural state do not like the cold, they have delighted botanists, and then gardeners, who have been able to cross them with northern plants to create new hybrid varieties growing in the gardens with the coldest European climates.

Right: *Lavandula* 'Hidcote' growing in a Mediterranean garden.

Below, left to right: Two of the lavender hybrids grown by the Filippi Nursery. 1. *L. lanata* cross-bred with *L. dentata* creates *Lavandula* x 'Goodwin Creek Grey'. 2. *L. multifida* crossed with *L. pinnata* gives *Lavandula* x *christiana*.

Italy also produces a small quantity of true lavender in Piedmont. It is mainly dried and used to fill scented sachets. Morocco is another land rich in lavender. All the varieties that grow in Spain can be found there, as well as others that are specific to the Atlas Mountains and surrounding hills. Botanists are still searching for new varieties in this area.

English mists in the land of the rising sun

Lavender, a plant originally from a hot climate, has nonetheless become one of the most familiar elements of the English garden, contrary to all that is known about their love of altitude, sun and dry soil.

This is perhaps nothing new, as the Romans probably introduced *L. angustifolia* to England. Other sources attribute lavender's introduction to the British Isles to Protestants from the Diois area, who fled to England with a few seeds in their pockets, just before the Edict of Nantes was proclaimed in 1598. There is no definitive proof of either theory. All that can be said with certainty is that by the end of the Tudor era, the herb gardens of grand houses and English monasteries counted true lavender among their medicinal plants. It was used to try to escape infection during contagious epidemics, especially in London during the Great Plague of 1665 – lavender was burned in churches and public places to disarm infectious fumes. In the nineteenth century, Queen Victoria was a wholehearted enthusiast, and ladies and gentlemen spread the scent that had become emblematic of

their native country throughout the Commonwealth. The refined perfume, English lavender, was born.

However, urban expansion in London overtook the oldest lavender fields, and since 1932 English lavender really only comes from one commercial farm of around forty hectares in Norfolk. From mid-July, true lavender and lavandin are gathered, distilled and used either for making eau de toilettes or dried to conserve their flowers. These products are available to those who visit England's lavender farms, who can admire the lavender gardens and the nursery.

English farms, almost all of whose dried lavender and lavender essential oil products are sold on site to visitors, do not rival French

professional cultivators who export a substantial amount of their production. The Crimea and Bulgaria exported lavender in the 1970s and 1980s, but political instability and economic complications in these countries led to a fall in production that is only just beginning to recover. Both cultivate lavender varieties from France, as the plant does not grow naturally in these countries. 'Maillette' and 'Matheronne', reproduced from cuttings, give high yields but of an oil that is less refined to the senses than seed lavender, which is closer to the wild plant.

The same varieties of lavender are grown in China today, in the northern province of Sinkiang on the Kazakhstan border, in a region that already specializes in producing essential oils.

Lastly, lavender has begun to be cultivated in Japan, mainly for the geometric beauty of its flowering fields. This initiative is due to the efforts of a seed merchant, Tadao Tomita, who, on a trip to France in 1970, bought lavender seeds in Marseille. He sowed these on the island of Hokkaido and newly-weds all rushed to have their photographs taken in front of the rows of flowering lavender. Today Tadao Tomita's lavender farm receives visitors from all over Japan and offers a variety of lavender products: eau de toilettes, bouquets, decorative objects, etc.

If the lovely Mediterranean plant has been able to adapt to growing in different parts of the world, it is thanks to a few botanists and to passionate gardeners, but also thanks to the knowledge of those who have cultivated lavender for generations.

A collection to visit

Olivier and Clara Filippi's lavender garden on the edge of Lake Thau is unique in France. They have managed to acclimatize around a hundred different varieties of lavender in a garden that is never artificially watered; their plants are only watered by the spring and autumn rains.

Top left: Originally from the Mediterranean basin, lavender has gradually spread to many other areas of the world. Lavender fields at Furano, on Hokkaïdo, Japan.

Left: Harvest time in a Norfolk lavender farm. Lavender is often grown in England where gardeners have created a multitude of horticultural varieties.

The garden seems dry at the end of summer, towards mid-August, but regains life with the first rains. All the botanical species of lavender that grow around the Mediterranean can be found there, as well as the varieties derived from them and the hybrids created by French and English gardeners. The frost-tender species from the Canaries and Cap-Verde are grown in a greenhouse.

All of these lavenders, lavandins and hybrids complement one another perfectly – a pale lavandin bush sets off a deep violet neighbour. Careful planting such as this creates a special ambience, born of colour and perfume associations, which vary in intensity at different times of the day.

In this garden the main flowering season is staggered from the beginning of June until mid-August, although a few isolated shrubs flower at the beginning and end of the season. From the beginning of April, some early-flowering plants like the Spanish lavender, *L. dentata*, start to display their spikes. The *L. angustifolias* point their inflorescences towards the south from mid-May and reach their best in June. 'Hidcote Blue', the jewel in the family's crown that comes from the famous English gardener Gertrude Jekyll's garden at Hidcote Manor, is a fragile beauty that dislikes damp. It is often replaced today by 'Folgate', which is easier to grow. This series, all of which are relatively small and generally more blue than purple, contains a few pink and white varieties with lovely but short-lived flowers – just like the true lavender from which they derive.

Some garden lavenders, from left to right:
• *Lavandula* x *intermedia* 'Super'
• *Lavandula* x *intermedia* 'Dutch', with campanulas in the foreground
• *Lavandula* x *intermedia* 'Hidcote White'
• *Lavandula* x 'Richard Gray'
• *Lavandula salvifolia*
• *Lavandula* x *intermedia* 'Seal' (foreground, left), *Lavandula* x *intermedia* 'Jaubert' (foreground, right), *Lavandula* x *intermedia* 'Abrial' (background)

In July, it is time for the lavandins, *L.* x *intermedia*, to take over with their longer flowering stems on bushes that are impressive by their size and for the number of flowers they carry. This hybrid, initially grown for the production of essential oils, has equally inspired gardeners and there are numerous varieties in the garden: 'Hidcote Giant', a majestic English shrub, and 'Alba', a tall variety with white-flowering spikes, are the most striking.

Lavenders from Spain and Morocco, *L. lanata* and *L. dentata*, underlie many varieties that combine the best qualities of the parent plants. These new hybrids are fairly hardy and have a long flowering season. Among the best, *L.* x 'Goodwin Creek Grey', the result of crossing *L. lanata* with *L. dentata*, has deep violet flowers from April to September.

In the garden, lavender is most often appreciated for its flowers, yet the measured rhythm of regularly structured plantings is never more visible than on a grey winter's day, when there is no colour in the mountains. And on some lavenders the leaves are more noticeable than their flowers. This is the case for two hybrids: *L.* x 'Silver Frost', which forms low-spreading clumps of ash-white woolly leaves, and *L.* x *intermedia* 'Dutch', a compact silver-grey ball that looks wonderful in a garden stripped bare by the winter.

Lavender gardens

Whether it covers an area the size of a handkerchief or a large expanse, a lavender garden offers delights that go far beyond the simple pleasures of gardening. It can be brought into the house in blue bouquets or potpourris, and it even brings a fresh original flavour to cooking. If lavender seems inescapable in any garden in southern France, where it reproduces the great blue flowering expanses of Haute Provence in miniature, it also has a special place in more northerly gardens, like those in England, where gardeners have demonstrated that passion, imagination and tenacity can produce miracles.

Wild and cultivated lavender varieties in Haute Provence are magnificent in quantity when their colours are spread over an open landscape. In a garden, however, these varieties can be disappointing, as they do not lend themselves to single or isolated planting. Of course, a couple of bushes will look attractive and grow well alongside thyme or savory in a corner of aromatic plants and herbs, but they are not the right plants to use in the foreground of a formal garden, especially as they have a fairly short flowering season. Dedicated botanically minded gardeners have improved on true lavender (*L. angustifolia*), creating numerous hybrids that are especially adapted for gardens, often with spectacular results. Today, the world of lavenders and lavandins offers an extraordinary diversity of forms, sizes and colours with a wide range of flowering times extending well beyond that of the field lavender. Their flowers come in many shades from white to dark purple, with lavender-blues, mauves and even pinks as well as the various shades of purplish violet offered by

L. angustifolia 'Twickel Purple'. One of them, the highly unusual *L. stœchas* 'Viridis' from Madeira, even offers green flower bracts.

The leaves of the plant, which are accorded little importance in cultivation, become an indispensable asset in the garden. At times green or a subtle grey-green, at times almost white and woolly, the evergreen leaves of lavender plants add interest to a winter border. The leaves are single and generally narrow, with straight or toothed edges, although in some species, such as *L. minutolii*, originally from the Canary Islands, they have such fine divisions that they look like feathers. Others have large composite leaves, especially many of the lavenders from North Africa and the Canaries, such as *L. multifida, L. pinnata* and *L. canariensis*.

On account of the shape and beauty of their leaves, these lavenders can be used for structural planting in the garden in the same manner as boxwood plants. They can be trimmed before flowering to form small round cushions, balls or informal shapely bushes. Some dwarf lavenders grow into small concentrated balls of blue flowers and others, whose flowering stems can measure over one metre in height, form less compact flowering clumps. Indeed, planting a few simple bushes in a couple of stone troughs carefully placed in one corner of a terrace will create a scene reminiscent of Provence, while a huge field of lavender brings wonderful colours and the scent of summer to a holiday home.

A little corner of Provence

The simplest and most spectacular way to grow lavender in the garden is to plant a border beside the house. It provides flowers and, when brushed against, gives off a wonderful scent that attracts bees and butterflies. It is low maintenance, with no need for watering, and will last well. Once a lavender shrub has taken root, it has a lifespan of at least ten years.

The stunning natural hybrid, lavandin 'Grosso', is perfect for this kind of planting. And why not combine two different varieties which flower

A key feature of a garden in the South of France, lavender shrubs also bring a Provençal flavour to gardens further north. Clumped together or used in a row, they structure the appearance of the ground in an original way and the bluish mauve of their small flowers beautifully offsets the pale yellow flowers of rose bushes, as here in the Viels-Maisons gardens in Picardy.

at different times, such as 'Super', a grey-blue lavandin flowering at the end of June, and the later-flowering 'Abrial'? It will extend the lovely lavender blues of the flowering season.

Simply trimming alternate lavender bushes in a row of plants creates a great effects with neat, round silvery-grey balls growing between unrestrained bushy violet tufts. Clipping bushes to create this kind of contrast is particularly effective for plants that grow where you can see them from the house. If your lavender grows outside a holiday home that you only use in high summer, lightly trim the bushes sometime in May, when the young spikes are just beginning to show – it will delay the main flowering season.

Lavender planted at the foot of trees in an olive grove looks especially attractive: blue plants under silvery trees! Both require little water and they grow well together, although the trees will need regular pruning so that they don't make too much shade for the lavender. This combination is frequently used by one of the most famous landscape architects in the South of France, Jean Mus. The scattered light of the olive trees gives the blue plant a dappled silvery shade that casts a changing light throughout the day. The effect is stunning. If you are lucky enough to own a home in the Mediterranean, you can create a successful composition with just a single olive tree – underplant it with three lavandins and a bush of *Rosa sinensis*, a perpetually flowering crimson dog rose.

In a desert garden, lavenders need to be combined with similarly plain plants. Spring-flowering cistus (sun rose), with their silky pink and purple petals, go particularly well with the first flowers of pale blue lavender. Large bushes such as these can form the architectural element on a bank, with a few delicate lavenders and some rosemary bushes slipped in lower down, bearing azure-blue and pale pink flowers, perhaps with the addition of a few miniature deep violet Provençal irises with yellow stripes.

Most lavender gardens are on chalky soil but a garden with acidic soil, that is only suitable for growing French lavender, can be made to resemble a lightly shaded woody glade, coloured from April by white-flowering cistus varieties, arbutuses and white-flowering tree heathers that exude the scent of honey. Such a woodland undergrowth is planted in the Rayol garden on the shores of the Mediterranean, landscaped by Gilles Clément at Rayol-Canadel-sur-Mer.

June-flowering lavender combines well with pale pink oenothera (evening primrose) that look like simple poppy flowers and move gently

Above: A clump of lavender, clematis and a white rose growing together against a woody backdrop, adding an air of colourful mystery to this garden.

Right: In a Mediterranean garden, thyme grows in front of the long-flowering stems of French lavender.

in the breeze, softening the rigid appearance of the lavender spikes. Bluish ornamental grasses, such as fescues or miscanthus, create a similar effect. Pale yellow achilleas (yarrow), with their flat heads of flowers carried high on tall stems, create a highly successful colour contrast with the mauve and violet bushes. Single-flowering oleanders form a similar contrast right at the height of summer when grown with late-flowering lavandin. As lavender repels ants and snails, this combination survives naturally without the need for chemical or biological treatment.

A combination of lavender bushes and ground-cover roses can transform a barren stretch of ground into a spectacular sight. Avoid pastel-coloured roses, and instead choose strong shades, such as carmine or magenta, that will offset the violet spikes. When the rose bushes are covered in flowers, the lavender is turning slightly blue, just enough to offset the colour of the roses, and when these are past their peak, the lavender comes into its own, the opulent violet clouds just highlighted by a few carmine-red or magenta flowers. Later, in winter, the silvery-grey lavender plants stand out from the rose bushes covered in bright red hips. An added benefit: as aphids dislike the smell of lavender, the rose bushes will always be healthy.

Lavandin never loses its country aspect and only acquires a more sophisticated allure when placed in the centre of a knot garden where a boxwood border contains its lavish flowering. It makes a perfect edging for an alley due to its tidy autumnal and winter shape, but remember to plant it well back from the edge of the path so that the long stems of the flowers don't block the way and make it difficult to walk around the garden in summer.

Lavender without a garden

Dwarf lavenders offer the possibility of patio gardening in large terracotta pots or stone troughs. A sunny balcony or terrace is sufficient space for a few bushes of *L. angustifolia*. The smallest, 'Blue Cushion', is less than 20 centimetres tall when in flower. 'Royal Purple', 'Munstead dwarf' and 'Erbalunga' do not grow much higher and offer a wide range of colours. Growing lavenders together with other scented plants enhances their fragrance, and, with an oleander in the background, it is possible, just for an instant, to believe you are in Provence.

Lastly, the wonderfully exotic tender lavenders, famed for their beautifully indented leaves, such as *L. multifida* and *L. pinnata*, lighten

Lavender, thyme, sage and oregano, all of which grow well in a dry rockery together, create a pleasant small garden of aromatic plants.

Previous pages: Lavender and roses soften the contours of a lawn in this Normandy garden.

and perfume pots of mixed flowers. They go well with multicoloured mixtures of summer annuals but like them, they only last a single season outdoors. The hybrid *L.* x *christiana,* which has unusually branched, dark blue flowering spikes, is the best variety to use in a hanging basket placed in a sunny, sheltered spot.

Outside the kitchen

Lavandula angustifolia grows happily beside other aromatic plants such as thyme, savory, blue-flowering hyssop, silver artemisia, the curry-scented helichrysum and the velvety leaves of sage bushes. Any plant with green leaves tending towards grey and silvery tones or white creates a good backdrop for lavender's blue and violet flowers. A subtle touch of yellow, as offered, for example, by a bronze fennel or the tall-flowering candles of mullein, very pale yellow on an almost white stem, is an essential element in the harmonious ensemble of this kind of garden. But be careful of such nuances of colour: a yellow that is too bold could be disruptive, and pale pink might appear insipid. On the other hand, dark ruby-red, or the purplish violets of an old rose sit well with the lavender's bluish tones. As a counterpoint, to balance the balsamic fragrances of these aromatic plants, the sweet smell of a Madonna lily or the refined scent of a damask rose, would be welcome additions.

A garden such as this provides lavender flowers that can be picked for cooking and for potpourris. Gathered in summer early in the morning and for immediate use, they can also be tied in small bunches, hung upside down and left to dry in a dark, well ventilated place. After a month, the flower, or more precisely its calyx, can be easily crushed between thumb and forefinger. When kept in a tightly sealed box, dried lavender retains all of its sensual properties from one summer until the next.

Growing lavender in the garden

Those who love this small blue flower dream of cultivating lavender in their own garden, whether the piece of land they own is in the South of France, elsewhere in the Mediterranean, such as Italy or Spain, or in England or another northern or central European country. Several hybrid varieties, adapted to wetter climates than that of southern Europe, make it possible to realize this dream. Generations of lavender growers have observed and adjusted the techniques so that everyone might possess a small lavender-blue corner in their garden.

Seeds, cuttings and plants

Creating a lavender garden is simple, as long as certain basic rules are respected. If there are no lavender bushes growing nearby, and you have no indication that your garden would support this type of plant, then a soil analysis should be made. Most lavender will only grow on chalky soil, and if the earth is too heavy, too acidic or lacks humus, it will need to be lightened, to have lime added and to be enriched with the necessary organic matter and manure.

Badly drained land and water that sits and stagnates around the roots during wet weather will cause the shrubs to rot very quickly as lavender bushes only like dry soil. In a hilly garden, they should therefore be planted in the upper half, and in a terraced garden they will need to be close to stone edges.

In places where winter is neither too cold nor too wet, lavender can be planted in autumn. Elsewhere they should be planted in spring, when the ground has started to warm up. Plants take root more easily if they are pot-grown. A bare-rooted plant, that is one that has been pulled up from the nursery, should be planted in the soil without delay and watered well.

In the fields, lavender is grown in rows with space left for the tractor in between – this usually means about 12,000 plants of lavender or 8,000 of lavandin, per hectare. In a garden, however, it is usually best not to plant in rows but to allow enough space between plants for them to spread, so that the flowering stems reach out and touch one another, covering the entire area. The result can be stunning; it is easily obtained with just three plants of lavandin or five of the slightly smaller lavender, per square metre.

Care is simple: hoeing in autumn, weeding in spring and cutting in summer which acts as pruning. A lavender garden takes three years to mature but then usually lasts for around ten years. The withering and decline that occurs in commercial cultivation is relatively rare in a garden setting.

Most stock of true lavender is grown from unselected seeds, which means the plants closely resemble the wild species and produce a range of shades. These plants need altitude to flourish; they need to feel the sun in summer and the cold in winter and will remain unharmed by snow or frost. There are nurseries that specialize in producing young plants from seed.

Nurseries also stock cloned lavender grown from cuttings such as 'Maillette' and 'Matheronne' that are well suited to the plains. Three

Above left: Lavender, which needs well-drained soil, can be grown in a pot. Here, *Lavandula* 'Cedar Blue'

Above right: A lavender shrub has a lifespan of around ten years and old plantations regularly need grubbing up and renewing as here, by taking slips from old stock.

lavandin varieties are generally available in garden centres: 'Abrial', 'Super' and 'Grosso'. Lavandin 'Super', which comes into flower from the end of June, resembles lavender and its floral essence is much less camphorous than the others. Lavandin 'Grosso', the most cultivated, is almost violet-blue from the beginning of July and its scent is a little heavy but lasts well. The 'Abrial' variety is the eldest. It flowers in July and its essence, famously refined, is fresh and lightly camphorous. There are many varieties available for planting to stagger the flowering times, each offering their own colour and fragrance in turn and providing bouquets for the house from June to August.

Lavender in the home

Bouquets and sachets

Using this small blue flower in the home is simply a question of bringing grandmother's ideas back into fashion. For example, adding a few drops of essential oil of lavandin to the final rinse water for cleaning the floor, using decorative blue bouquets in small woven baskets, or a well placed potpourri can scent the entire house, creating the happy and carefree atmosphere of summer fields in Provence.

Scents of yesteryear and the smell of cleanliness

Lavender was important in the days when only natural products were used to maintain domestic hygiene. Lucienne Roubin recounts this seasonal ritual of the *bugade*, or the first spring clean, in *Le Monde des Odeurs*:

"Once all the items have been placed, a hemp sheet is centred on top of everything with its edges overhanging the sides of the vat. A bed of fine ash especially created for the purpose and carefully sieved is added in the middle. Finally, the flowers of a large bunch of lavender, picked the previous summer, are lightly strewn over it. The edges of the sheet are gathered up and folded on top and the operation is ready to begin. The washing starts, that is to say, boiling water is poured over the lot. But the sheets are only taken to the washing place on the following day."

Once the sheets have been folded and ironed, lavender is again used in cupboards and laundry presses: small scented sachets filled with clean lavender flowers are used to combat mites, repel ants and other insects and to scent the linen. Because lavender essential oil does not stain, a few drops may be added to a towel or a pillowcase to scent the entire cupboard.

Such traditional usage of lavender can inspire other means of scenting linen sheets, embroidered cloths and woven hand towels: a few drops of essential oil of lavender added to the rinse water gives the linen a fresh fragrance, as can using lavender hydrolat which is sometimes sold as surplus by distilleries. Packaged by the half-litre, this scented ironing water is relatively expensive. It can be replaced by adding a few drops of essential oil to the demineralized water in the iron; in this case, always use true lavender (*angustifolia*) oil as lavandin is not sufficiently subtle for use on clothes. Lavandin oil, on the other hand, is excellent for rinsing the floors. Ten drops added to five litres of warm water brings a fresh, clean smell to the bathroom or kitchen. Try cleaning tiles in the old-fashioned way, using products based on soft soap and lavandin essential oil.

For a subtle and original way of scenting a room, place crushed flowers of true lavender in a bowl. Revive them regularly by adding a few drops of essential oil. Alternatively, create a simple potpourri of lavender flowers mixed with damask rose buds, whose colour and fragrance work best with true lavender.

Fragrances that circulate can be used in combination with such localized fragrances. Use a diffuser for this. Available from shops selling essential oils, they just take a few drops of essential oil. These can be mixed to form lovely blends and suitable fragrances for summer or winter: a blend of five drops of essential oil of bergamot, five of verbena, two of geranium and two of lavender (*officinalis*) creates a fresh, light scent that is extremely pleasant in summer. In the cold season, try eight drops of essential oil of mandarin, four of cinnamon and four of lavender (*officinalis*) to create a warm, cosy ambience.

Selecting room fragrances is a delicate matter: heavy sweet scents should be avoided, as they are the antithesis of good-quality lavender oil, which is both herbal and floral, but dry.

Blue patience, blue passion

The art of making bouquets, dollies and embroidered lavender sachets calls for ancient know-how, passed down through the generations during long hours of dedicated work. The widespread tradition of plaiting dollies or spills has disappeared, as they take a long time to make and require

Right: Lavender flowers are used to scent linen folded on the shelves of an inherited armoire. Sachets of lavender flowers, hand-embroidered by Édith Mézard at the Château de l'Ange, at Goult, in the Lubéron.

Below: Plaited lavender dolly of the type used to scent linen in the past.

meticulous attention to detail. The people of Provence used their agile fingers to plait long lavender stems that needed to be fresh so as not to break and the dollies could therefore only be made at harvest-time. Thirty spikes were tied together with a bit of raffia, quite close to the flower heads. The stems were wound round in such a way as to enclose the flowers and then woven together: the sprigs of lavender forming the warp, and violet and mauve ribbons the weft, passed over, under…

Today, hand-embroidered linen, like plaited lavender dollies, has unfortunately become a rarity. Édith Mézard still embroiders by hand in her workshop, and families that hold linen in high esteem still order their children's trousseau from her: blue lavender flowers are finely embroidered into each corner of white or coloured linen tablecloths, and white lavender flowers onto beautiful grey linen. Good seamstresses can embroider their own linen, highlighting the delicacy of this plant motif, and haberdasheries now stock beautiful lavender-themed patterns – bouquets, alphabet samplers and delightful replicas of antique botanical illustrations.

Like embroidery, writing is a time-consuming activity …

"Yesterday I read of the nature of the circumstances in a manuscript that smelled sweetly of dried lavender and was marked with gossamer threads…"

The opening lines of Alphonse Daudet's novel, *La Mule du Pape* (The Pope's Mule) inspire one to write. Why not leave a few sprigs of lavender to dry in a favourite book or in a box of mauve or blue handmade writing paper? Alternatively, you could perhaps perfume some violet ink by adding a few drops of essential oil. Such fragrant letters will not pass unnoticed, especially if a few flowers fall out as the lavender-coloured *billet-doux* is opened by its recipient!

Right: To make this lovely turned bouquet, you need three small bunches of *lavendula angustifolia* 'Super-blue', a handful of ears of wheat and… incredible dexterity.

Below: Lavender incense sticks.

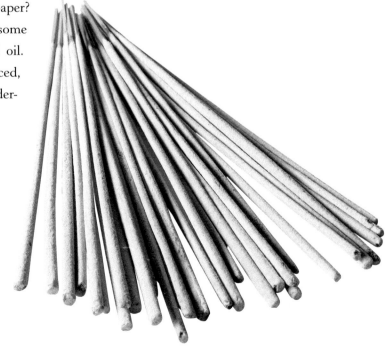

90

Cooking with lavender

Two ways of breathing the scent of lavender into the centre of a plate…

Left: Lavender jelly, used during the preparation of lavender mousse.
(RECIPE PAGE 115)

Below: Aromatic lavender oil.
(RECIPE PAGE 105)

Blue is a colour rarely found among fruits and vegetables. In food, it is often recognized as a warning sign. Lavender did not naturally find itself on our plates on account of its colour but has been brought there by the current vogue for eating flowers. Today's food lovers relish nasturtiums, marigolds and lavender… Daring to add this small flower to the culinary repertory and learning to use it with delicacy adds a distinctive, original and elegant flavour to festive dishes and winter recipes.

Lavender should be used in moderation. It is a highly aromatic herb with a "rich flavour that can anaesthetize the senses," explains Yves Gattechaud, whose restaurant in Provence has for years presented a menu completely dedicated to delicate lavender flavours. He recommends that, "it is better to use fine lavender. Some lavandin varieties contain too much camphor and for most of us, that smell is associated with medicine rather than the pleasures of the table. As well as that, heating quickly gives it a bitter quality." Jams are the only exception – in this case the flowers are added after cooking as the jam is poured into jars.

Essential oil of lavender, on the other hand, has a powerful aroma and is generally kept out of the kitchen, except when closely following the advice of an innovative and audacious chef.

Quantities vary according to individual preference and to the quality of the lavender. Dried flowers are easy to use in all preparations but it would be a shame not to savour the unique flavour of freshly picked lavender. When using fresh flowers, the amount indicated should be doubled, but it is best to experiment. Whether cooking with fresh or dried flowers, ensure that they are organic or, better still, from your own garden. The commercial lavender grown in large fields is not cultivated for culinary use, and the flowers usually contain pesticides and fertilizers.

Sweet lavender, savoury lavender

There are various methods of acquiring or extracting lavender's aromatic flavours. One of the best ways to do this is to infuse the flower for a few minutes in milk or cream, which is heated but never brought to the boil, as it would turn bitter. To achieve the desired flavour, the scented infusion should be tasted after three and then five minutes. It needs to be filtered before being used.

Another method adds the flowers directly to the dish that is being prepared. To flavour meat, for example, flowers are added when deglazing. At that time a little bit of good vinegar balances the lavender's scent and compensates for its sweetness. The flavour of the plant goes particularly well with lamb, chicken, rabbit and goat.

For summer barbeques and grills, a mixture of four-fifths thyme flowers and one-fifth lavender flowers, or olive oil aromatized with lemon thyme and lavender, tastes delicious and brings an unexpected twist to the classic aromatic herb of Provence.

For subtle sweet flavouring, use lavender honey whose flavours are enhanced rather than damaged in cooking. When buying, it is worth knowing that a few weeks after the honey has been put in a jar it naturally crystallizes, becoming fairly thick and almost creamy and opaque. Its characteristics are a refined texture in the mouth and flavours reminiscent of the flower. Colour varies from creamy white to golden yellow, it is slightly acidic and the fragrance explodes in the mouth. Liquid honey is almost certainly the result of reheating after crystallization and carries the risk of being distorted, and of losing some of the quality of its taste and character.

Right: Only the flowers of lavender are used in cooking, fresh or dried.

Below: Lavender is delicious in combination with sun-ripened fruits, such as figs or (as here) peaches, especially in jams and tarts.

Tomato and lavender jelly
with herb fritters

Serves 4

FOR THE TOMATO JELLY:
1kg (2lbs) ripe beef tomatoes
2 gelatine leaves, softened
1 tsp fresh lavender flowers

FOR THE LAVENDER VINAIGRETTE:
500ml (18fl oz) white wine
or cider vinegar
1 tsp fresh lavender flowers
2 drops lavender essential oil
A handful of red summer fruits
500ml (18fl oz) olive oil
200ml (7fl oz) water
Salt and pepper

FOR THE HERB FRITTERS:
60g (2½oz) flour
10g (⅜oz) cornflour
7g (¼oz) baking powder
Around 120ml (4fl oz) iced water
A few fresh lavender spikes
A few fresh sage leaves
A few fresh thyme flowers
Oil for deep-frying

Make a fritter batter by mixing the flour, cornflour and baking powder, then slowly pouring the iced water in while beating to form a thick creamy consistency. Set aside to rest at room temperature. Meanwhile make the tomato jelly. Skin, deseed and purée the tomatoes. Put them into a heavy saucepan and add the gelatine and the lavender flowers. Simmer on a low heat; do not allow to boil. Sieve the hot mixture to remove the flowers and pour it into four small moulds. Leave them to chill in the fridge for at least three hours.

To make the vinaigrette, bring the vinegar to the boil. Remove from the heat and add the lavender flowers, essential oil of lavender, summer fruits, olive oil and water. Season with the salt and pepper, leave to cool, then bottle.

Just before serving, dip the herbs into the batter and fry in boiling oil. As soon as they turn a pale golden colour, lift them out with a slotted spoon and place on kitchen paper to drain.

Take the tomato jellies out of their moulds, serve with the herb fritters and drizzle some lavender vinaigrette on top to season.

This light summer recipe comes from Yves Gattechaud.

Starters

Lubéron leek tart

Serves 4

250ml (9fl oz) crème fraîche

1 tbsp dried lavender flowers

4 leeks

30g (1oz) butter

Salt and pepper

3 eggs

FOR THE SHORTCRUST PASTRY:

150g (5oz) flour

A pinch of salt

75g (3oz) butter

2 tbsp water

Gently heat the crème fraîche in a pan, but do not allow it to boil, then add the lavender flowers and leave to infuse for 5 to 7 minutes. Wash and slice the leeks. Heat the butter in a frying pan, add the leeks and gently sauté them over a low heat for about 10 minutes. Season with salt and pepper. Beat the eggs into the sieved lavender cream, then add the leeks.

To make the shortcrust pastry, rub the flour, salt, butter and water together in a mixing bowl. Wrap the dough in foil or a polythene bag and leave to chill in the fridge for 20 minutes before using.

Heat the oven to 200 °C. Roll out the pastry and line a pie or quiche dish. Pour in the leek mixture, then place in the oven. Lower the heat to 180 °C and bake for 30 minutes, or until done. Serve hot.

Recipe from Olivier Etcheverria's book, *La Lavande, dix façons de la préparer.*

Iced melon soup with olive oil and lavender flowers ›

Serves 4

4 small Canteloupe melons

3 tbsp olive oil

1 tbsp fresh lavender flowers

Salt and pepper

Slice off the top third of the melons and scrape out the seeds. Using a melon baller, dig out twenty balls from the flesh and refrigerate. Carefully hollow out the remaining flesh and blend with the olive oil. Place the empty melon shells in the freezer.

Add the lavender flowers to the melon-oil-mixture. If the consistency of the soup mixture is too thick, add a little water. Season with salt and pepper.

Place the mixture in the freezer for an hour. Serve the soup in the hollowed out frozen melon shells arranged on a plate of crushed ice. Garnish with the melon balls.

Recipe created by Bénédicte Appels, La Maison du Moulin in Grignan.

Pigeons and cherries with lavender

Serves 4
30g (1oz) butter
1 tbsp olive oil
2 pigeons
Salt and pepper
500g (1lb 2oz) cherries (stoned)
1 level tbsp fresh lavender flowers
20ml (¾fl oz) sherry vinegar
20ml (¾fl oz) Marc de Provence (or brandy)

Heat the butter and the oil in a shallow, heavy dish or pan. Add the pigeons, season with salt and pepper and gently fry for 10 to 15 minutes. Cut pigeons in half and keep warm.

Add the cherries and cook rapidly in the juices. Sprinkle with a few lavender flowers. Add the vinegar. In a spoon, warm the Marc de Provence, set alight and pour into the pan. Put out the flames immediately.

Return the pigeons tp the pan and reheat for 2 minutes with the cherries. Serve with steamed green beans.

Quick recipe byYves Gattechaud.

‹ Lavender chicken

Serves 6
1 tbsp olive oil
40g (1½oz) butter
8 pieces of grain-fed chicken
8 shallots
2 level tbsp flour
150ml (5fl oz) fresh chicken stock
150ml (5fl oz) red wine
Salt and black pepper
4 sprigs thyme and, if possible, a few thyme flowers
2 tsp dried lavender flowers

Heat the oil and butter in a cast iron pot. Add the chicken pieces and lightly brown, then set aside.

Peel and gently fry the shallots in the chicken fat.

Add the flour to the pan and cook gently for 2 minutes, stirring with a wooden spoon. Slowly add the stock and the wine, as if making a béchamel sauce.

Season with salt and pepper and return the chicken to the sauce together with the thyme and lavender. Simmer over a low heat for 30 minutes.

Serve with Creole-style basmati rice.

Meat dishes

Roast goat with lavender

Serves 4

1 leg of young goat (boned),
about 800g (1¾lb)

Salt and Szechuan pepper

50ml (1¾fl oz) of Marc de Provence
(or brandy)

8 spikes of lavender

2 sprigs of wild thyme or flowering
garden thyme

100ml (3½fl oz) olive oil

3 garlic cloves

4 slices of French country bread

Season the inside of the leg with salt and pepper and sprinkle with the brandy. Place the lavender and thyme in the centre of the meat. Roll up the roast and tie it securely with string. Baste liberally with olive oil.

Roast on a spit for about 40 minutes, basting frequently for best results. Peel and halve the garlic and rub the bread slices with the garlic. Halfway through cooking, place the bread on the dripping tray under the roast to soak up the juices.

Serve with new potatoes.

Leg of lamb with lavender honey

Serves 4

50ml (1¾fl oz) olive oil

Salt and Szechuan pepper

1 leg of lamb, about 2kg (4½lb)

1 heaped dessertspoon of mixed
lavender and thyme flowers

500g (1lb 2oz) small onions or
shallots

4 tbsp lavender honey

Oil and season the leg of lamb and sprinkle with the flowers. Preheat the oven to 220 °C. Place the lamb in the oven, lowering the temperature to 180 °C after 10 minutes. Roast for 50 minutes (40 minutes if you like your lamb 'pink'), basting frequently. Peel the onions or shallots. Halfway through cooking, add them to the dripping tray under the meat. About 10 minutes before the end of the cooking time, heat the grill, pour the honey over the roast and leave to caramelize before switching off the oven. Leave the meat in the oven with the door open to rest for 5 minutes before serving. Serve with stoned halved apricots, seasoned with pepper and lightly sautéed in butter.

Sisteron barbequed lamb kidneys ›

Serves 2

6 lambs kidneys

100ml (3½fl) oz aromatic olive oil
infused with lavender
(RECIPE PAGE 105)

Fresh lavender flowers

Wooden skewers, barbeque or
charcoal fire

Salt and pepper

Prepare the kidneys by slicing them in half lengthwise and cutting out the fatty part in the centre with the tip of a sharp knife. Sprinkle with aromatic oil and leave at room temperature for 30–60 minutes.

Thread the kidneys onto the skewers then sprinkle with lavender flowers and grill for 2 minutes on each side.

Season with salt and pepper and serve with freshly buttered pasta.

Lavender butter

Lavender butter

125g (4½oz) unsalted butter

1 tbsp lemon juice

1 level tbsp chives

1 level tbsp of chervil

2 tsp fresh lavender flowers

Soften the butter by placing it in a bowl over a pan of boiling water or by heating in a microwave for a few seconds on low power. Finely chop the herbs and the lavender, then mix into the butter with the lemon juice, using a fork. Roll the mixture into a sausage shape and cover with aluminium foil. Place in the fridge for a few hours then serve the lavender butter with fresh steamed vegetables.

Onion and honey lavender preserve

Makes around 500ml (18fl oz)

1.5kg (3½lb) small new onions

500g (1lb 2oz) cooking apples

1 unwaxed lemon

1 garlic clove

1 shallot

300ml (10fl oz) water

350 (12fl oz) aged red wine vinegar

1 tsp powdered cinnamon

4 tbsp lavender honey

Salt and pepper

Peel and halve the onions. Peel the apples, remove the core and pips, then dice. Grate the zest, and squeeze the lemon, retaining the juice. Peel and roughly chop the garlic and shallot. Place the ingredients in a heavy bottomed-steel pan, adding the water. Bring the mixture to the boil, lower the heat and simmer for 20 minutes.

Add half of the vinegar and continue to simmer gently for 20 minutes. Add the rest of the vinegar and the cinnamon mixed with the lavender honey.

Mix and continue to stir with a wooden spoon while cooking for another 20 minutes, until the mixture forms a marmalade consistency. Pour into hot jars as when making jam. This preserve keeps for several months.

Serve cold to accompany roast leg of lamb or roast pork.

Lavender-growers' sauce

Makes 400ml

(14fl oz or about ¾ pint)

6 shallots

300ml (10fl oz) chicken stock

1 level tbsp dried crushed lavender flowers

Salt and pepper

Finely chop the shallots. Pour the stock into a heavy bottomed pan and add the shallots and the lavender. Season to taste.

Simmer over a low heat until the shallots soften. This sauce, served hot, makes a delicious accompaniment to with roast veal or pork.

A traditional recipe from the Forcalquier area in the Alpes-de-Haute-Provence.

Sauces and accompaniments

Aromatic lavender oil ▲

Makes 500ml (18fl oz)

500ml (18fl oz) Nyons olive oil

A few sprigs of fresh lemon thyme

2 tsp fresh lavender flowers

Pour the olive oil into an attractive bottle that can be used at the table. Add the herbs and lavender and leave in a dark place to infuse. The oil is ready to use after around 15 days and goes perfectly with grilled meats such as lamb chops, kidneys and fine sausages.

Blackcurrant and lavender wine sauce

Makes 200ml (7fl oz) sauce

150ml (5fl oz) dry (not acidic) white wine

A handful of blackcurrants

A pinch cornflour

2 tsp fresh lavender flowers

Salt and pepper

Make the sauce to accompany a roast. Add the white wine to the dish in which the meat has been cooking and stir with a wooden spoon to dissolve the juices. Add the blackcurrants. Bring the mixture to the boil over a high heat, dilute with a little water, add the lavender flowers and thicken with the cornflour. Season.

Served hot, this sauce is a perfect accompaniment for leg of lamb or duck breast.

Recipe by Yves Gattechaud.

Lavender jelly

Makes 500ml (18fl oz) jars

1.8kg/4lb cooking apples
2 level tbsp fresh lavender flowers
1.5l (2½pints) lavender water
(hydrolat/floral water)
1.3kg (2lb 12oz) sugar
Fresh lavender flowers to decorate

Peel and roughly dice the apples. Retain the seeds and put them in a small muslin bag that will be cooked with the apples and removed when cooking is done: their pectin helps to thicken the jelly.

Place the apple, lavender flowers and hydrolat into a jam-making saucepan or large pan, and cook over a high heat until the mixture forms a purée.

Empty the purée into a jelly bag (or a thickly woven dishcloth that you can wring out) and leave to drip, collecting the juice in the pan.

Measure the quantity of juice obtained and add 1kg (2¼lb) sugar per 900ml (1½pints) juice and bring to the boil. The jelly is ready when a drop placed on a cold plate stays firm.

Pour the hot mixture into sterilized jars adding a few lavender flowers to decorate. This can be used like quince jelly, served on toast.

‹ Preserved hot figs with lavender honey and ice cream

Serves 4

18 fresh purple figs
1 level tbsp castor sugar
1 vanilla pod split in two
1 cinnamon stick
2 tbsp lavender honey
300ml (10fl oz) red wine
250ml (9fl oz) vanilla ice cream

Place the figs in a large cast-iron pan, sprinkle with sugar, add the vanilla and cinnamon and pour the honey on top.

Cook over a low heat for 30 minutes. Cover with the red wine and continue simmering over a low heat for a further 30 minutes.

Serve hot in shallow dishes, together with a spoonful of vanilla ice cream or natural yoghurt.

Sweets and Desserts

Raspberry jam with lavender

Makes 4 or 5 jars of 500ml (18fl oz)
2kg (4½lb) of raspberries
1kg (2¼lb) preserving sugar
1 tbsp lemon juice
2 level tbsp fresh lavender flowers

Tip the raspberries, without washing them, into a bowl and add half of the sugar. Cover with a dishcloth and leave them to stand all night at room temperature. Next day, collect the juice and bring to the boil with the rest of the sugar, stirring frequently.

Add the raspberries to this syrup together with the lemon juice and boil (removing any scum) for 15 minutes. Remove from the heat and add the lavender flowers. Mix, pour into jars and seal.

Peach jam with lavandin ›

Makes 8 jars of 500ml (18fl oz)
3kg (7lb) yellow peaches
3kg (7lb) granulated sugar
Small bunch lavandin flowers

Scald the peaches in hot water. Peel, remove the kernels and chop the flesh into small pieces.

Cover the fruit with the sugar and stand for 3 hours at room temperature. Bring to the boil and cook over a high heat for 30 minutes, stirring frequently.

Place 3 lavandin flower spikes in the bottom of each jar before pouring the boiling jam on top. Seal in jars while hot.

Lavender apples

Serves 4 to 6
1kg (2¼lb) small autumn apples
90g (3½oz) caster sugar dissolved in
100ml (3¼fl oz) water
10g (⅜oz) extra caster sugar
1 stick cinnamon
1 tsp dried lavender flowers
30ml (1fl oz) aged rum

Peel the apples and place side by side in a large pan. Cover with the sugared water. Add the extra sugar, cinnamon and lavender flowers. Cover and cook over a low heat until the apples are soft. Remove them from the pan and reduce the juices to syrup.

Arrange the apples as 2 or 3 layers in a mould and pack well down. Cover the apples with the syrup, pour the rum over and set alight. Serve these apples with a simple pound cake or sponge fingers.

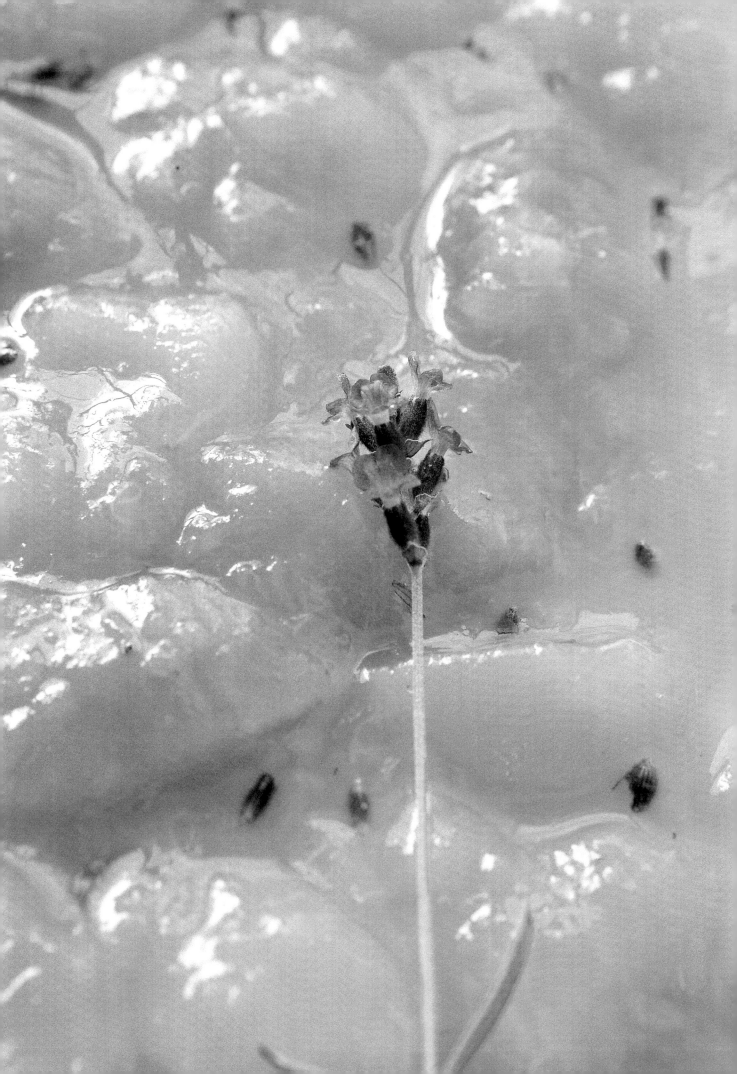

Lavender-flavoured strawberry dessert

Serves 4
800g (1¾lb) highly aromatic
strawberries
50g (2oz) caster sugar
30ml (1 oz) kirsch or cooking sherry
2 tsp fresh lavender flowers

Place the strawberries in a large fruit salad bowl and cover with sugar, drizzle over the kirsch and sprinkle with lavender flowers.
Allow the mixture to stand in a cool place for 24 hours, then serve chilled.

Apricots with lavender honey ›

Serves 4
8 apricots
8 tbsp lavender honey
250ml (9fl oz) pistachio ice cream
1 lavender sugar (RECIPE PAGE 113)

Preheat the oven to 180 °C. Halve the apricots and remove the kernels. Place each apricot half on a baking sheet, pour over half a tablespoonful of honey and bake for 10 to 15 minutes.
Serve hot with a large spoonful of pistachio ice cream and with an orange and lavender thin to decorate. (SEE RECIPE PAGE 113)

Peach and lavender flower tarte tatin

Serves 4
4 yellow peaches
1 tsp dried lavender flowers
75g (3oz) diced butter
75g (3oz) caster sugar

FOR THE SHORTCRUST PASTRY:
150g (5oz) flour
Pinch salt
75g (3oz) butter
2 tbsp water

Skin the peaches, remove the kernels and dice the flesh. Crush the lavender flowers.
Scatter half of the butter over the bottom of a deep sandwich tin, add the lavender flowers and cover evenly with half the sugar.
Pack the peaches tightly into the tin, with the rounded side facing down. Distribute the rest of the diced butter and the sugar over the top. Cook the peaches to caramelize over a low heat.
To make the shortcrust pastry, rub the flour, salt, butter and water together in a mixing bowl. Wrap the dough in foil or a polythene bag and leave to chill in the fridge for 20 minutes before using.
Preheat the oven. Roll out the pastry to cover the peaches, tucking it in all around. Cook in a moderate oven for 25 to 30 minutes.
Remove from the tin and serve warm.

Orange and lavender thins

Serves 4 to 6
200g (7 oz) melted butter
450g (1lb) icing sugar
The juice of 2 oranges
2 tsp dried lavender flowers

Combine the melted butter, icing sugar, orange juice and lavender flowers to form a cream. Leave to cool for a few minutes before rolling out on a non-stick surface.

Place in a moderate oven for 6 to 7 minutes. As soon as it starts to turn a nice caramel colour remove it from the oven. Let the mixture cool for a moment, then remove it from the non-stick surface with a spatula before it hardens. Form the thins by delicately lifting the outer edges to curl.

Cool and serve with ice cream or chocolate mousse.

Created by Claude Broquin, pastry chef at the Hostellerie du Val de Sault.

Caramelized lavender flowers

For 300g (10½oz) of lavender
flowers
30g (1oz) glucose
250g (9oz) caster sugar
120ml (4fl oz) water
1 bouquet of fresh lavender flowers

Melt the glucose, sugar and water in a pan and continue heating until the caramel turns pale yellow.

Remove from the heat and, one by one, dip the lavender spikes in the caramel mixture. Place on baking paper to dry.

Store the lavender flowers in a tightly sealed container and use them to garnish desserts.

‹ Nougat ice cream with lavender honey

Serves 4
75g (3oz) sliced almonds or
pistachios
75g (3oz) assorted candied fruit
125g (4½oz) thick, chilled crème
fraîche or double cream
30g (1¼oz) caster sugar
3 tbsp lavender honey plus 2 more
tbsp for pouring
2 tsp water
3 egg whites
Fresh lavender flowers to decorate

Brown the almonds or pistachios lightly in a dry pan without oil. Finely chop the candied fruit. Whip the crème fraîche until it doubles in volume, then add sugar to taste.

In a small pan, stir the honey into the water, bring to the boil and remove from the heat.

Separate the eggs. Beat the egg whites until stiff, slowly adding the hot honey syrup in a thin stream. Gently stir in the almonds, candied fruit and whipped cream. Pour the mixture into a bowl and freeze for at least an hour.

Serve with a drizzle of honey. Lavender honey is often thick; it may need to be heated to become liquid. Decorate with fresh lavender.

Honey and lavender ice cream

Serves 4
300ml (10fl oz) single crème fraîche
or single cream
6 spikes of fresh lavender
4 egg yolks
30g (1¼oz) caster sugar
2 tbsp lavender honey
300ml (10fl oz) thick crème fraîche or
double cream
fresh lavender flowers to decorate

Bring the crème fraîche to the boil in a pan, remove from the heat and add the lavender flowers for a few minutes.

Beat the egg yolks and sugar to form a creamy mousse.

Bring the crème fraîche mixture back to the boil and pour through a sieve into the egg mousse. Beat well.

Pour the mixture into a saucepan and cook over a low heat, stirring with a wooden spoon until the cream coats the spoon. Stir in the honey and leave to cool.

Whip the thick cream and fold into the lavender cream. Place in an ice cream maker. Serve, decorated with lavender flowers.

Lavender and peach sorbet

Serves 4
1.5kg (3½lb) peaches
30g (1¼oz) dried lavender flowers
200g (7oz) caster sugar
450ml (16fl oz or ¾ pint) water

Skin and stone the peaches then purée the flesh. Add the flowers and leave to infuse for 3 minutes, then filter.

Bring the sugar and water to the boil to make a syrup, then mix with the peach purée and place in an ice cream maker.

Recipe by André Sube, pastry maker in Vaison-la-Romaine.

Lavender crème brûlée

Serves 4
4 eggs
100g (4oz) caster sugar
500ml (18fl oz) crème fraîche
1 tbsp dried lavender flowers
4 tbsp Demerara sugar

Bring the crème fraîche to the boil and remove from the heat.

Add the lavender and allow to infuse for 5 to 8 minutes. Taste the mixture and strain when you feel it is sufficiently flavoured.

Beat the egg yolks and caster sugar until the mixture forms a thick creamy mousse.

Continue beating while adding the hot filtered cream. Pour into individual, oven-proof dishes and cook in a moderate oven for 30 minutes then allow to cool.

Before serving, sprinkle with the Demerara sugar and caramelise quickly under a hot grill or with a burner.

Mousse with lavender flowers ▲

Serves 4

3 gelatine leaves
or 6g (¼oz) agar-agar
100g (4oz) soft brown sugar
100ml (4½fl oz) water
2 tsp fresh lavender flowers,
and a few to decorate
500ml (18fl oz) single cream

Soak the gelatine with the sugar in the water. Bring to the boil, remove from the heat, add the lavender, and cool. Strain after 5 to 7 minutes.

Whip the cream and fold into the warm mixture.

Divide between individual dessert dishes and chill for 2 hours.

Serve the mousse decorated with lavender flowers and an apricot coulis, if liked.

Venaissin Lavandine

Serves 4
500ml (18fl oz) curds, preferably
from Rove goats' milk
1 pot thick-set yogurt
3 tbsp thick crème fraîche
5 tbsp lavender syrup (RECIPE BELOW)
1 tbsp fresh lavender flowers

Whip the curds to break up the lumps, add the yogurt and continue beating. Add the crème fraîche and mix well.

Add the lavender syrup; sweeten according to taste with the honey and mix.

Divide the mixture between small bowls, add a few flowers then leave the lavandines to chill for 24 hours before serving.

Recipe from Claudine Vigier, cheese maker at Carpentras.

Drinks

Infusion 'le Mâle'

Serves 4
500ml (18fl oz) mineral water
2 tbsp fresh lavender flowers
5 leaves fresh mint
1 tsp orange flower water
1 tsp vanilla extract
Lavender honey to sweeten

Bring the mineral water to the boil. Add the lavender flowers and mint leaves and leave to infuse for 10 minutes before straining.

Add the orange flower water and the vanilla extract, then sweeten with lavender honey.

(PHOTOGRAPH PAGE 126.)

Recipe taken from *La Lavande, dix façons de la préparer* by Olivier Etcheverria.

Lavender cordial ›

Makes 1 litre (1¾ pints)
A handful fresh lavender flowers
1 litre (1¾ pints) mineral water
250g (9oz) lavender honey
(adjust quantities according to taste)

To prepare the lavender flowers, separate them from the stems, then leave them to marinate in the mineral water for 12 hours.

Strain the water and add the lavender honey, heating gently to dissolve.

Chill in the fridge. Serve chilled or with lavandine du Venaissin (RECIPE ABOVE).

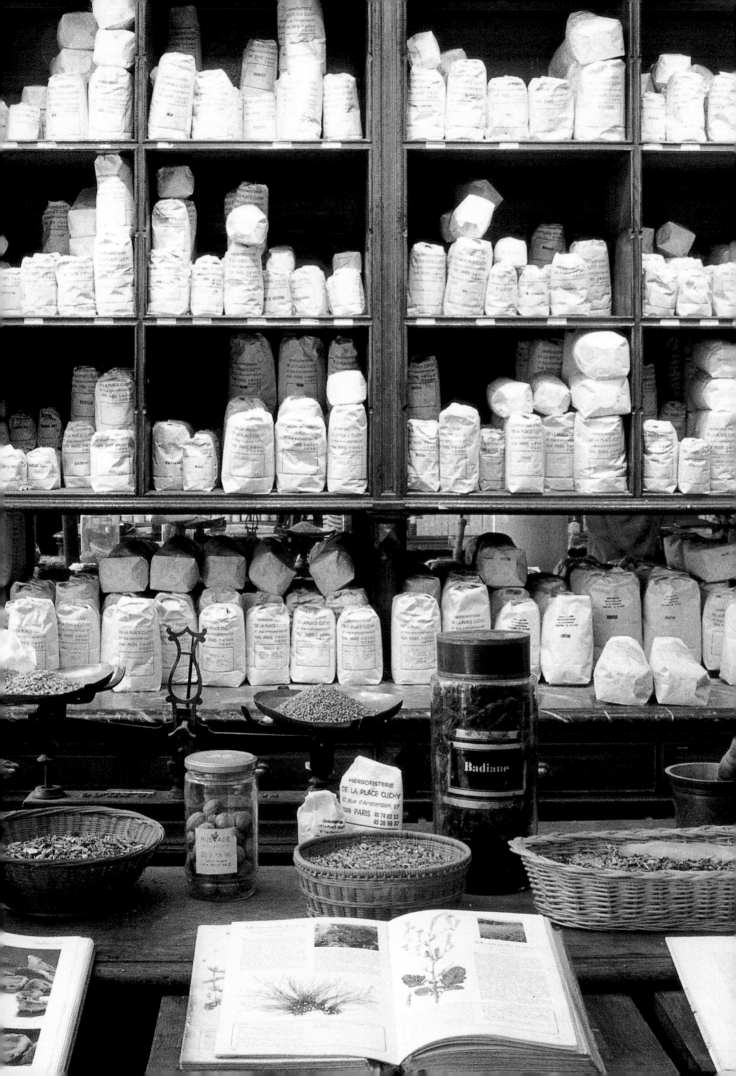

Old and new remedies

Left: Lavender, treasured by herbalists, holds pride of place on the shelves of any shop selling herbs. Herbalist shop in Place Clichy, Paris.

Below: A physician, wearing a beaked mask filled with sweet-smelling herbs including lavender. It was thought to act as a protection against the plague. Eighteenth-century chalk drawing.

Physicians and botanists have been familiar with the scent of lavender and the therapeutic values of the plant for hundreds of years. Both spike and French lavender are mentioned by Pliny the Elder in his *Natural History* and by Dioscorides in his *Materia Medica*. Both considered them to be precious medicinal herbs. During the Middle Ages, lavender was believed to be a miracle cure – those who worked in the perfumeries remained protected from infection during plague and cholera epidemics thanks to lavender's antiseptic, antibacterial and even antiviral properties.

A miraculous remedy

One anecdote, which has become legendary in France, is that of the "four thieves' vinegar" which took place during the plague years of 1628 to 1632. It tells of four brigands who knowingly robbed victims of the plague, without fear of contamination. The story, documented in the archives of the courts of Toulouse, tells of the four thieves who "decided to go into the homes of people sick with the plague, to strangle them in their beds and to steal from their houses, remaining unharmed by the pestilence". The ingenious robbers revealed their secret – they oiled their skins with an aromatic herbal preparation and even gave the recipe: equal parts of lavender, absinthe, rosemary, sage, mint and rue, macerated in camphorous white wine vinegar.

During the eighteenth century, the hospice at Carpentras was famous for its snake cure, regarded as a supreme remedy for use in severe illness. It contained up to 47 different ingredients, including Florentine irises, ginger, cardamom, pimento, cinnamon, opium and Indian spikenard… Locally grown saffron, fennel and particularly lavender were added to these rare and costly items. The mixture, thickened with Spanish wine and Narbonne honey, was only prepared once a year, blessed and then presented with great ceremony to the local people who considered it a truly miraculous cure-all. It was kept for dosing only those who were gravely ill and guaranteed, sometimes, an astonishing recovery.

Thus, lavender has come down through the centuries, surrounded by the reputation of being an almost miraculous plant. To put it more modestly, during the nineteenth century and until relatively recently, it has been the singularly most important remedy in the first-aid boxes of everyone living in Provence.

Grandmother's medicine cabinet

Country people in Provence are very familiar with the values of the natural world around them; they know which wild plants are edible and which have medicinal properties. At the end of the eighteenth century, the medicinal use of lavender was not the preserve of specialists. There were only a few doctors in the countryside – and the knowledge of the plant's healing powers had been simply handed down from generation to generation through the centuries.

Until the twentieth century, true lavender was often the only medicine of the Provençal shepherd who left home in the summer to spend long solitary months with his animals. Lavender enabled him to treat the saddle sores of the ass, to disinfect wounds, as well as the umbilical cords of newborn lambs and, by so doing, to facilitate healing. He used essential oil of lavender to cure the viper's bite on his dog's nose, to get rid of ticks and to alleviate the pain of hornet stings. To rid his dog of fleas, he only had to ensure it slept on lavender bedding, which repulses most insects, but not bees.

In the home, too, essential oil of lavender was a general remedy for all ills. An application cooled burns, taking away the pain and rapidly accelerating healing. Lavender was also employed to calm itchy insect bites. As a hair wash, it was a remedy for lice – apply some essential oil to the scalp and leave for twenty minutes before rinsing. The lice should disappear! Lavender hydrolat was added to the final rinse after washing hair as a preventative measure.

A drop of essential oil, taken on a sugar lump, apparently eliminated worms. In winter, when colds and bronchitis seemed imminent, mothers would rub a few drops of lavender essence

Left: Used from the Middle Ages up until the nineteenth century, the snake cure was a universal remedy made from plants, minerals and sometimes powdered snake pounded together in a mortar. Its composition varied depending on which region the cure-all came from (here, Venice). In Carpentras, a fair amount of lavender was included in the mixture. *Growembroch*, an eighteenth-century manuscript from the library of the Correr Museum, Venice.

Right: Before herbalists and pharmacists, apothecaries prepared and sold dried herbs, powders, oils and other plant-based creams. Wood engraving from *Das Buch der Cirurgia*, Strasbourg, 1747.

on their children's chests, before tucking them in at night. Inhalation with lavender flowers, often combined with thyme, soothed the bronchial tubes when a cough threatened. Mothers used to calm over-excited children by rubbing a drop of essential oil of lavender on their temples or by slipping a sachet of the dried flowers under their pillows. The elderly mixed a few drops with a neutral carrier oil and used it to massage painful joints and to soothe muscular cramps and contractions.

The medicinal power of lavender has been discovered gradually, in an empirical manner: its prophylactic effect was observed in the animals that slept on lavender-straw bedding, and its ability to promote scarring and the rapid healing of nicks, cuts and gashes from the sickle could be seen on the hands of old lavender gatherers.

A living treasure

Recent molecular studies of lavender and its beneficial powers confirm how well founded its traditional uses were: the plant is anti-spasmodic; promotes the formation of scar tissue; is anti-inflammatory, anti-allergenic, anti-rheumatic, it is an antidote to venom and an insecticide... Innocuous, it can be used externally without risks. It should only be used internally, that is to say, the essential oil should only be ingested, in precise regulated doses, under the guidance of a qualified practitioner.

Lavender is always in the news, usually with regard to the development of complementary medicine that recommends the use of plants. Dried lavender flowers are used for infusions and inhalations. Aromatherapy uses essential oils to bathe, to massage skin or to inhale a large 'breath of lavender-scented air'. Essences of lavender are used: *angustifolia*, spike lavender, lavandin or a combination, depending on the effect desired. Lavender *angustifolia* essential oil is anti-depressive, calming and a little exhilarating, that of spike lavender is stimulating and toning, while lavandin combines the best of both as it calms while maintaining a certain stimulus. Choice depends on the time of day and on the season – true lavender is more for winter and spike lavender more for summer use – and on personal preference.

Lavender *angustifolia* flowers and herbal medicine

Medicinal herbalism is not a new science – the use of herbs to promote healing is well documented throughout the ages, and this science was probably practised long before that. For generations lavender recipes designed by the Ancient Egyptians and the Romans, then by Provençal country folk, have been improved and refined and some of these thousand-year-old remedies are still in use today.

Today, whether drinking an infusion of lavender flowers or breathing in their vapours during inhalation, it is important to know how the lavender was grown and how it should be stored. Indeed, only organic lavenders or those with a certified guarantee of origin (AOC) can be certain of not being toxic. To ensure their properties remain intact, bleached flowers should be kept in a tightly sealed box, away from air and light, and renewed each summer during the harvest.

For a good night's sleep, take a herbal infusion of two teaspoons of dried flowers of lavender *angustifolia* in a mug of hot water. Sweetened with lavender honey, to alleviate the acidic taste, it will make a delicious soothing drink.

Lavender tea is one of grandmother's delicious remedies – as long as it is not left to infuse for more than three minutes, after which it becomes bitter.

A herbal tea made with mixed dried lavender flowers, lemon balm and marjoram is soothing after a meal as it aids digestion: simply place a teaspoon of each into a pot, add boiling water, allow it to stand for five minutes, then pour.

When colds are prevalent, a steam inhalation of lavender flowers combined with eucalyptus flowers, both excellent antiseptics, is a wonderful remedy. This simple old family recipe is one of the most successful: scatter a tablespoon of lavender flowers and another of dried leaves into a basin filled with extremely hot water. Stir, then, placing a towel over your head and the bowl to concentrate the vapours, hold your face over the steam and breathe deeply.

Lavender essential oils and aromatherapy

Essential oils of fine lavender, spike lavender and lavandin contain extremely concentrated, active and effective elements, and therefore need to be used with care. Rodolphe Baltz, author of *Les Huiles essentielles, comment les utiliser* (*Essential oils and how to use them*), notes that they should never be brought into contact with the eyes and that before use, you must ensure there is no allergic reaction by placing a single drop on the back of the wrist and waiting a few hours. Once some simple precautions have been taken, you can gently and easily look after your health and well-being with massages, rubs, relaxing baths, inhalations, and by using diffusers.

Essential oil of lavender *angustifolia* is particularly suited to the way we live today. Soothing and relaxing, it is one of the best essential oils for combating stress: simply apply a few drops of wild lavender *angustifolia* on the insides of the wrists and on the solar plexus and rub gently to calm yourself. The essential oil penetrates the outer layer of skin and just by this simple contact, the whole body benefits from the properties of the oil.

Using a diffuser or burner, which breaks down the essential oil into millions of tiny droplets, is one of the best ways of preventing bronchial problems from the beginning of winter. Lavender *angustifolia* can be combined with eucalyptus or thyme to provide a natural and efficient means of disinfecting and destroying air-borne microbes.

For colds, a steam inhalation over a large bowl of hot water to which are added two drops each of essential oils of sage, pine and lavender *angustifolia* is a great decongestant. A small handkerchief scented with a dozen drops of the slightly camphorous essence of spike lavender will aid breathing.

Frequent travellers should always keep a small bottle of essential oil of lavender with them. Smelling the scent helps to take the stress out of flying – in fact, many commercial anti-stress travel kits include it. On arrival, try a hot bath containing six drops of essential oil of lavender *angustifolia*, two of marjoram and two of geranium for a good night's sleep, despite the time difference.

Lavandin essential oil is a good first-aid remedy for numerous small summer ailments and injuries. To make an excellent remedy for healing insect bites, add 150 drops of geranium essential oil and 150 drops of lavandin to 10ml of alcohol warmed to 70 °C. Place a few drops on the affected area and massage lightly with the tips of your fingers and the painful sensation will ebb away. Lavandin essential oil is good for sunburn too: a cold bath to which several drops have been added, followed by an application of lavandin-impregnated compresses to the burnt parts of the body, will reduce redness and swelling. A few drops of essence of lavandin, directly applied to small burns, will lessen pain and help the skin to heal.

After cramping or muscle fatigue, a massage oil made as follows is truly relaxing and soothes the pain: 150 drops each of essential oils of lavandin and rosemary diluted in 10ml olive oil.

Choosing and storing essential oils

There are some quality guidelines to bear in mind when choosing a lavender essential oil.

Seventy tonnes of lavender *angustifolia* are produced each year for the perfume industry, to make luxury fragrances, cosmetics and aromatherapy products. Most of the 1,180 tons of lavandin essential oils are produced for the manufacture of washing powder and products. Naturally enough, the manner in which they are distilled depends on the use that will be made of them. In oils destined for aromatherapy the molecular composition of the lavender is of primary importance, whereas in the perfume industry, the fragrance or scent of the oil comes first.

The analyses made to determine the quality of the essential oils are fairly well developed. Their scent, of course, is taken into account but so too is their colour: pale yellow for lavender, darker yellow for lavandin. Laboratories also carry out chemical and physical analyses: today, chromatography separates the different constituents in an extremely precise manner.

Right: Lavender oil massage, a pleasant and effective way to relax.

Below: Antique perfume bottle designed to conserve lavender essential oil away from the light.
(Musée des Arômes, Saint-Rémy-de-Provence)

Above: Nineteenth-century
label of essential oil of
lavender.
(From the collection of
Lucien Vakanas)

Left: The infusion "le Mâle"
is a combination of lavender,
fresh mint, vanilla and
orange flowers.
(RECIPE PAGE 116)

A bottle of good-quality essential oil will be clearly and precisely labelled, indicating the variety of the lavender and its Latin name: *Lavandula angustifolia* for true lavender (English lavender), *L. latifolia* for spike lavender and *L.* x *intermedia* for hybrid lavender or lavandin. With regard to the latter, the fact that they are grown from cuttings or 'cloned' is interesting, as their perfumes vary. If lavandin 'Grosso' can be said to have a lasting, almost heady scent, then lavandin 'Super' can be said to be more floral and less camphorous. As for lavandin 'Abrial', its fresh, lightly camphorous fragrance is a fairly refined scent.

A guarantee of quality can offer additional assurance: an organic label guarantees that the oil is produced from a plant grown without pesticides and following a lengthy distillation that respects the integrity of the properties of the plant. From 1981, true lavender has had its own AOC appellation, 'Huile essentielle de lavande de Haute Provence', awarded only to to lavender grown from seed in high-altitude plantations, including a geographical zone limited to the specific area located in the Alpes-de-Haute-Provence, the Hautes-Alpes, the Drôme and the Vaucluse. Each year the lavender has to meet rigorous criteria. Wild lavender *angustifolia* picked at altitude, sometimes over 1,200 metres, is both rare and costly, but for passionate lavender lovers it offers the pleasure of a real "scent of angels". Essential oil keeps for two to three years. It should be bottled in dark-coloured glass (usually blue or brown) or stored out of the light and the top should always be properly sealed. High temperatures of 30 °C (86 °F) or above, especially when exposed for prolonged periods, can damage the composition of essential oils and alter their properties.

Lavender beauty secrets

In the world of health and beauty, lavender is in a league of its own, whether used as an essential oil, a hydrolat or simply as fresh or dried flowers. Synonymous with purity, fresh air and sunshine, it offers a simple, familiar and natural form of care with the power to calm while toning and stimulating every part of the body.

All of nature's graces

In countless cosmetic products, particularly those containing only vegetable or organic ingredients, lavender essential oil acts both as a fragrance and as a preservative. It offers an efficient and natural ingredient instead of the synthetic compounds and artificial ingredients that are often used. Lavender is also used to make hydrating face creams with a green tea or magnolia base, and to make skin repair creams, using a cocoa butter base.

On its own, lavender is generally used in skincare products for oily skin and it is particularly suitable for young people with skin problems: lavender hydrolat or floral water is a fantastic cleanser and helps to detoxify the skin. A few drops of lavender vinegar, gently dabbed onto the problem areas of the face with a cotton bud or cotton wool, is great for healing spots. Lavender shampoo, made by adding a few drops of essential oil to your usual brand, helps greasy hair to maintain health and balance. Gentle rinsing with floral water will keep your hair shiny for longer.

Even more importantly, lavender provides a means of combining beauty care with a pleasant sense of well-being in everyday body care and hygiene tasks such as washing, massaging moisturizing creams into the skin, freshening up, etc.

TEMPLE BAR.

Six bunches a penny, Sweet blooming Lavender !

A global beauty product

In the USA, lavender is exceptionally popular. In many toiletry and beauty care products it is presented as a pleasing, simple remedy for treating daily problems. It is a real relaxation programme that's on offer, from lavender bubble bath to lavender body milk.

In Britain, on the other hand, lavender beauty products are presented in an almost austere manner. Bottles and containers bear neutral-coloured labels that list the composition of the content in its entirety. These discreetly herbal-scented products are usually made exclusively from vegetable ingredients and do not contain preservatives, so there is no fear of allergic reactions, even from the most delicate skin!

In Greece, many natural beauty products hark back to an old tradition of combining lavender with the products of beekeeping – honey and royal jelly – in various hydrating and relaxing skin creams.

Thus, in every country, lavender symbolizes a return to simple, traditional ways of cleansing and maintaining hygiene. The French beauty industry is not alone in seeing this plant gradually becoming more prevalent in its creations. Many cosmetic companies were born beside fields of lavender and aromatic and scented plants. Hence Sanoflore manufactures essential oils, floral waters, bath products and other body creams near Vercors and in Provence. This company, which only works with organic essential oils, is where the idea originated of drawing up a register of responsibilities and duties for those specializing in organic beauty products, the Cosmébio label.

Occitane, located close to the fabled plant reservoir otherwise known as the Montagne de Lure, only uses ingredients derived from plants and the certified *huile essentielle de lavande de Haute Provence (AOC)* (Haute Provence lavender essential oil) in the different products of its lavender range. Such close proximity between lavender fields and beauty products is the mark of an increasing desire to preserve and value the plant in its most natural and original state.

Launder yourself!

"Lavender… to bathe in lavender… to wash. In French, 'se lavander' meant to wash and in English, *a lavender* was a laundress. To lave in Middle English was to wash oneself as it is in French today – je me lave… Philosophers, grammarians and a few pedants have said that lavender is called lavender because its name comes from *lavando*, gerund of the Latin verb lavare (to wash). Some have disagreed. Others give all sorts of explanations. But it just isn't true. Lavender has always

Right: Advert for Yardley's *Old English Lavender*, a lavender-scented eau de Cologne created in 1873. Brought to France from England around the turn of the twentieth century, it was fashionable for a considerable time.

Below: Molinard's *Les Fleurs de Provence*, a lavender eau de toilette made by this Grasse perfume manufacturer.

Yardley's
Old English
Lavender

AT the Dance, the Theatre, the Cabaret Show and wherever the charm of Perfume adds to the joy of the moment, Yardley's Old English Lavender is sure to be the dominant note. Its beautiful clean fresh fragrance has been cherished by the Leaders of Taste and Fashion for over a Century. A lovely Old-World Perfume, it has always been fashionable and is always in good taste.

Charming as it is as a perfume—it is yet more than a perfume and has wider uses:

IN HOT AND CROWDED *assemblies, a little sprinkled on your handkerchief and applied to the skin is deliciously cooling and invigorating and will restore the fresh daintiness of your appearance.*

WHEN FATIGUED AND HEADACHY *after shopping or during long motor or railway journeys, a little applied to the face is cleansing and delightfully soothing and refreshing.*

IN THE SICK ROOM *there is nothing which will so effectively cleanse and freshen the atmosphere and make it agreeable to Patient, Nurse and Visitors.*

IN THE HAND BASIN *a few drops will delicately perfume and soften the water and its beautiful fragrance will linger on the skin long after use.*

AND LASTLY *when home, tired after an evening's enjoyment—the luxury of a little in your bath.*

PRICES: 1/10, 3/-, 5/-, 8/6, 10/6 and 21/-

THE LAVENDER PERFUMERY also includes :—Toilet Soap, 3/- (box of 3 large Tablets); Face Powder, 2/6; Talcum Powder, 1/2; Face Cream, 1/6; Bath Salts Tablets, 3/-; Shampoo Powder, 1/6; Sachets, 1/6

From all Chemists, Coiffeurs, Departmental Stores and from

YARDLEY, 8 NEW BOND STREET, W.1

been called lavender. And because it refined fresh water and made the sun's rays seem more pleasant, and as it became indispensable to those who wanted to get rid of the charms of the night", from their linen and on their bodies, "that it was habitually used in the morning, with sun and water and therefore it became said, 'I am using lavender' – I lavender, I lave, I launder."

In his book, *Célébration de la lavande*, Jean Bouvier humorously underscores these intimate links between lavender and the act of washing. The source of the word is of little importance as long as one takes pleasure in… laundering oneself! Like Jean Bouvier, let's celebrate lavender in a series of simple magical rituals.

Using lavender hydrolat in a spa bath creates an extraordinary sensation of relaxation. Five or six litres poured directly into spa water will not create any kind of problem for machinery. In winter, adding a few drops of essential oil of lavender *angustifolia* or lavandin in the water for making steam in the sauna makes a pleasant change. Essential oils have begun to be used in some health spas and an extremely hot lavandin bath followed by a massage with essential oil of lavandin is deeply relaxing and ensures an incomparable quality of sleep. At home, it is easy to make an old-fashioned salt bath by tipping a large bottle of coarse sea salt into the bottom of the bath and adding 20 drops of lavandin or lavender. Run the bath as hot as possible to ensure relaxation. The scent of the lavender will fill the bathroom, creating a soothing and calming sensation.

Sleep is an enduring beauty secret. Massaging the solar plexus with two drops of lavender essence promotes a rest and relaxation filled with images of the colour blue. A few drops of lavender essence in a vaporizer or burner in the bedroom, is an exquisite prelude to entering the land of dreams.

Bring the warmth of summer into the depths of winter with a lavender-scented candle, a cup of green tea sweetened with lavender honey and a neck and shoulder massage using sweet almond oil with lavender essence (100 drops of essence to ten millilitres of sweet almond oil).

One perfume, many perfumes

"Lavender: a fresh, fairly lively note. A perfume floral without being heady, a green note that is not bitter. It's sparkling, fresh, floral but without being sweet: it's often used as a top note."

This is how Robert Ibanez, who creates fragrances for Robertet, a perfume company in Grasse, describes lavender. He is a *nez* (the term

Right: Beauty products made by Durance, a company established right at the centre of the Drôme lavender fields, whose products are mainly based on this plant.

Below: Mauve lavender soap, coloured to indicate the plant whose fragrance it contains.

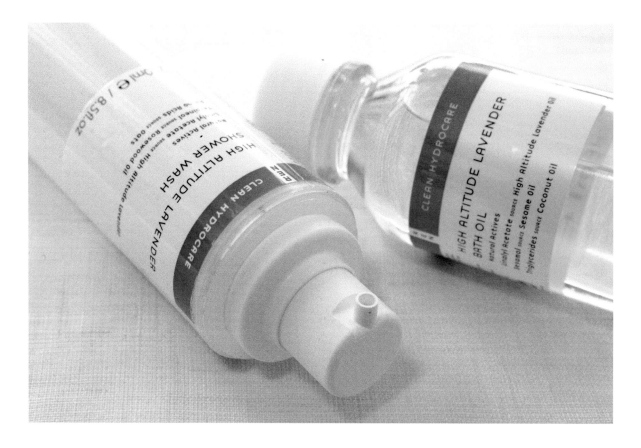

for one of the highly qualified perfume creators, meaning literally a 'nose') and invented *Pure lavender*, for Azzaro, by blending lavender with notes of musk, wood and amber.

Only lavender from the best sources, carefully distilled from high altitude plants grown from seed in Haute Provence, are used as a natural ingredient by the famous perfume companies. The Florentine *aqua mirabilis* fragrances, created from citrus fruits and rosemary essences, form the basic compositional elements of today's lavender eau de Colognes: The fresh, herbal combination of rosemary, bergamot and sometimes lemon essences are harmoniously blended with the lavender. The final notes in this sequence were added at the end of the nineteenth century by the Yardley company who used lavender, rosemary, spike lavender, eucalyptus and bergamot as top notes in combination with middle notes of clary sage, geranium and cedar and base notes of oak moss, Tonka bean and musk to make *English lavender*. Since then, all lavender eau de Colognes have been created around the same type of blend, perhaps adding a little more lemon, petit-grain, basil or a hint of artemisia.

Houbigant's *Fougère Royale*, created in 1880, is a harmonious blend that combines lavender with woody base notes. It has been adapted by

Above: Bath and shower gel with true lavender (*angustifolia*) grown at high altitude made by the American company REN.

Right: Origin's face cream with essential oil of *Lavandula angustifolia*.

134

numerous modern men's perfumes. The amount of lavender has been reduced but it is still there. Guerlain's enduring fragrance *Jicky*, created in 1889, or *Mouchoir de Monsieur*, created in 1904 and dedicated to the city dandy, made lavender a very Parisian flower. Caron's 1934 perfume *Pour un homme*, remains a bestseller. The fashionable boyish women of the roaring twenties adored it, and women still steal it from the men in their lives.

Thanks to the Osmothèque, it is possible to journey back in time and discover some of the perfumes of the past. This perfume conservatory, located quite close to the palace of Versailles, recreates long-lost fragrances with the collaboration of retired nez. It is both wonderful and astonishing to be able to smell Napoleon's lavender Cologne and Habanera, created for the great French couturier Paul Poiret.

From the 1970s, lavender became less fashionable, confused with the scent of lavandin in washing powders, but a few more recent creations

Left: At the beginning of the
twentieth century, although
lavender water was mainly
used by men, it was often
given to babies too.
(From the collection of
Lucien Vakanas)

Below: Antique bottles
of lavender water.
(Musée des Arômes,
Saint-Rémy-de-Provence)

have revived its popularity. In 1995, *Le Mâle*, from Jean-Paul Gaultier, blended the scent of lavender with that of cinnamon and orange flowers and, like *Pour un homme*, it is as pleasing to women as men. Diptyque's *Eau d'Élide*, created in 1988, which marries bitter orange zest and wild lavender, musk and aromatic plants, actually recreates the scent of sunbathing in Provence. The wonderfully restrained *Lavande*, by Annick Goutal, created in 1981, is a masculine fragrance with a touch of smoke. The *Eau de toilette à l'huile essentielle de lavande de Haute Provence de l'Occitane*, which first sold in 2000, is self-evident – the scent of a lavender field in flower.

Lavender is present everywhere, in ritual beauty care and memories of ancient miracles, in daily skincare products and fragrances created by large perfume companies, a blue perfumed link between traditional and creative invention, between simplicity and luxury, health and beauty, and above all between humankind and nature.

Address book

Associations and guides

THE LAVENDER BAG
English Lavender magazine
with botany, history and
information on amazing places
that grow lavender.
Tel: +44 (0) 115 989 2718
www.headfamily.freeserve.co.uk

MAS DES LAVANDES
Jeanne-Marie Pascal offers an
ethno-botanical discovery of
the history of lavender.
Gîte available for holidays.
Hameau-de-Fonssargoules
84210 Venasque - France
Tel/Fax: +33 (0) 4 90 66 00 58
www.mas-des-lavandes.com
jmpascal84@wanadoo.fr

POIVRE D'ÂNE
Tour the lavender paths on the
back of a donkey in the Alpes-
de-Haute-Provence, near
Digne.
La Bastide des Férauds
04380 Thoard - France
Tel: +33 (0) 4 92 34 87 12
poivre.ane.free.fr
poivre.ane@free.fr

LES ROUTES DE LA LAVANDE
This association promotes the
land where lavender is
cultivated. Each year it edits
brochures in French, English
and German that devise
suggested itineraries around
the lavender theme and provide
details of contacts such as
farms, distilleries, shops, etc.
Good for reference…
2, avenue de Venterol
26110 Nyons CEDEX
France
Tel: +33 (0) 4 75 26 65 91
Fax: +33 (0) 4 75 26 32 67
www.routes-lavande.com

SABRINA DA CONCEICAO
Experience and learn all about
fine lavender and lavandin near
Contadour and at the remote
dry stone sheep pens as

Sabrina da Conceicao takes you
along the paths of the
Montagne de Lure.
Rue des Braves
04870 Lincel - France
Tel: +33 (0) 4 92 76 66 23
sabrinagdp@free.fr

VAGABOND'ÂMES
Sébastien Mesnières offers
walking tours of the Baronnies
and relates the history of
Mévouillon 'Super-blue'…
Tel: +33 (0) 4 75 28 50 48

Museums

MUSÉE DES ARÔMES
Marvellous collection of
antique perfume bottles.
Attractive distillery and shop
at the museum entrance in
August.
34, boulevard Mirabeau
13210 Saint-Rémy-de-Provence
France
Tel: +33 (0) 4 32 60 05 18
Fax: +33 (0) 4 32 60 17 16
www.florame.com
florame@florame.com

MUSÉE DE LA LAVANDE
DU COUSTELLET
The history of distillation is
revealed through a collection
of antique stills, from portable
to steam equipment.
Route de Gordes
Hameau du Coustellet
84220 Cabrières d'Avignon
France
Tel: +33 (0) 4 90 76 91 23
Fax: +33 (0) 4 90 76 85 52
www. museedelalavande.com

MUSÉE DE LA LAVANDE
DE SAINT-REMÈZE
Exhibition of antique copper
stills and demonstration of
old distillation techniques in
summer. Shop and library.
Departmental highway 490,
direction the Ardèche gorges.
07700 Saint-Remèze - France

Tel: +33 (0) 4 75 04 37 26
Fax: +33 (0) 4 75 04 23 66
www.ardechelavandes.com
info@ardechelavandes.com

OSMOTHÈQUE
Make an appointment to
experience perfumes from
olden days in this perfume
school.
36, rue du Parc-de-Clagny
78000 Versailles - France
Tel: +33 (0) 1 39 55 46 99

Places to stay
in the lavender fields

AUBERGE RURALE DU MOULIN
Located at the foot of the
Montagne de Lure, this inn
makes an ideal base for
exploring mountain villages like
Banon and Simiane-la-Rotonde.
04230 Lardiers - France
Tel/Fax: +33 (0)4 92 73 38 54

LE CHÂTEAU DE LA GABELLE
Rooms are available in this
fifteenth-century guesthouse
surrounded by fields of wheat
and lavender. Marguerite Blanc,
a passionate lavender grower,
demonstrates lavender cutting
and shows visitors how to make
bouquets and plaited lavender
dollies…
26570 Ferrassières - France
Tel: +33 (0) 4 75 28 80 54
Fax: +33 (0) 4 75 28 85 56
www.chateau-la-gabelle.com
chateaulagabelle@wanadoo.fr

LA FERME TUSHITA
A rustic house which offers
guestrooms opening onto small
fields of true lavender and
breathtaking views of the Mont
Ventoux.
Route d'Aleyrac
26230 Salles-sous-Bois
France
Tel: +33 (0)4 75 53 55 16
Fax: +33 (0)4 75 53 62 98

LA FORGE-SAINTE-MARIE
Located in Eygalayes, one of
the smallest villages in France,
the house is in a calm, quiet
area and has a lavender spa.
Guided walks of the area are
also on offer.
26560 Eygalayes - France
Tel/Fax: +33 (0)4 75 28 42 77
isabelle.muse@wanadoo.fr

LES GÎTES DE DANY
ET JEAN-LOUIS FIOC
In a magnificent old farm, a
couple of young agriculturalists
who love to share their passion
welcome visitors wishing to
stay in a place surrounded
by cultivated aromatic plants
and lavandins.
Quartier Daliers
26130 Montségur-sur-Lauzon
France
Tel: +33 (0) 4 75 98 12 02
Fax: +33 (0) 4 75 98 09 58

LA MAISON DU MOULIN
This refined guesthouse on
the bank of a small river is a
perfect base for exploring the
countryside around Grignan.
You can also learn about
cooking with lavender.
Quartier Petit-Cordy
26230 Grignan - France
Tel: +33 (0) 4 75 46 56 94
Fax: +33 (0) 4 75 46 50 34
www.maisondumoulin.com
info@maisondumoulin.com

Lavender farms

BEAR CREEK LAVENDER FARM
Revealing the passion
Americans have for lavender,
this is a recent creation that
had its first harvest in 2003.
P.O. Box 63660
Pipe Creek, Texas 78063
USA
Tel: +1 (0) 830 510 6800
joy@bearcreeklavender.com
www.bearcreeklavender.com

**BLUE MOUNTAIN
LAVENDER FARM**
An island of colour created by 3,000 lavender bushes in the middle of wheat fields. This Franco-American family cultivates six varieties. Lavender flowers are sold fresh and as bouquets.
345 Short Road
Touchet, WA 99360 - USA
Tel: +1 (0) 509 529 3276
Fax: +1 (0) 509 522 3276
info@bluemountainlavender.com
bluemountainlavender.com

CLAYBANK FARM LAVENDER
Pati and Doug Mathias studied how to grow and use lavender in France and now cultivate it in their fields and nursery. They offer a range of bath products.
610 Boothe Road - Naramata, BC V0H 1N0 - Canada
Tel: +1 (0) 250 496 5788
info@claybankfarmlavender.com
www.claybankfarmlavender.com

LA FERME DE LA BAUME ROUSSE
Different themed visits are available in this agricultural holding: botany; watercolour painting; relaxation in the spa.
Marion Haas
26400 Cobonne - France
Tel: +33 (0) 4 75 25 08 68
Fax: +33 (0) 4 75 25 39 30
www.lafermedebaumerousse.net
info@lafermedebaumerousse.net

LA FERME BRIN D'HERBE
In his farm, Bénédicte Delpit offers workshops aimed at children: plant walks; sensory games; distillation; and jam tasting.
Quartier les Collins
26460 Bézaudun-sur-Bîne
France
Tel: +33 (0) 4 75 53 37 12
lescollins@mageos.com

JERSEY LAVENDER LIMITED
This lavender farm belonging to the Christie family is designed for visitors, lavender is cultivated, harvested by hand

and distilled. Essential oils, eaux de toilette, flowers and edible lavender specialities are on sale.
Rue du Pont-Marquet
Sainte-Brelade - Jersey
Channel Islands
Tel: +44 (0) 153 474 2933
A good internet site for a virtual visit:
www.jerseylavender.co.uk

LIZ ET MAX PATMOY
At 2 hectares planted with 24,000 lavender plants, this is the largest lavender farm in New Zealand. All its products are environmentally friendly. The essential oils, whose exact composition is given on their internet site, are mainly used in aromatherapy.
527, Napier-Taupo Highway
Hawkes Bay – New Zealand
Tel: +64 (0) 68 36 65 53
Fax: +64 (0) 68 36 66 64
Numerous interesting links about lavender are available on the internet site:
www.whitebay.co.nz

NORFOLK LAVENDER
Lavender farm designed for visitors.
Caley Mill Heacham
Kings Lynn
Norfolk PE31 7JE - Great Britain
Tel: +44 (0) 148 557 0384
www.norfolk-lavender.co.uk

SONOMA LAVENDER
True lavender cultivated on the Pacific shore. Lovely range of bath and beauty products. Spa products.
420 B Tesconi Circle
Santa Rosa CA 95401 - USA
Tel: +1 (0) 707 523 4411
Fax: +1 (0) 707 523 4466
www.sonomalavender.com
gary@sonomalavender.com

TOMITA
Huge lavender fields at the heart of a farm wholly dedicated to flowering plants, at the foot of Mount Tobachi on Hokkaido in Japan. You can

take part in distilling. A shop sells lavender perfumes, bath products, lavender honey and lavender tea.
Hokusei, Nakafurano-cho
Sorachi-gun
Hokkaido 071-0704 - Japan
Tel: +81 (0) 167 393 939
Fax: +81 (0) 167 393 111
scent@farm-tomita.co.jp
www.farm-tomita.co.jp

Distilleries
open to the public

Although large modern distilleries are not open to the public on account of the dangers linked to the comings and goings of lorries, the heat and difficult working conditions, the small traditional distilleries, on the other hand, are happy to welcome curious passing visitors.

DISTILLERY BLEU PROVENCE
Philippe Soguel is a perfect teacher who likes to share his passion and his job with the public. If you have a little lavandin in your garden, this is the only distillery where you can bring it to be distilled and gain the proud honour of having your own personal bottle of essential oil. Sells essential oils.
Promenade de la Digue
26 110 Nyons - France
Tel: +33 (0) 4 75 26 10 42
Fax: +33 (0) 4 75 26 15 90

**DISTILLERIE DE LA GRANGE
DE LA TATINE**
Visiting this organic agricultural business in summer will give you a full understanding of lavender from the seed to plant and you can take part in distilling.
Le Village
26510 Chauvac - France
Tel/Fax: +33 (0) 4 75 27 87 87

DISTILLERIE DU VALLON
This distillery is right in the middle of the blue Plateau de Sault. In August, when it is

open to visitors, the distillers willingly explain their work.
84390 Sault - France
Tel/Fax: +33 (0) 4 90 64 14 80

LE PRÉ DU JAS
One of the smallest stills in the South of France, it operates in August in the mountains near Nyons. On the 15 August, at the annual village fête, the distiller and producer, Bernard Ducros, operates the still for all those curious to see how it works. Sale of organic essential oils.
26510 Villeperdrix - France
Tel: +33 (0) 6 75 16 34 57

Visiting gardens,
where to buy lavender

DOWNDERRY NURSERY
This nursery sells the best selection of lavender cultivars from papillon lavender for acid soils to lavenders from the Canaries and frost-hardy plants…
Simon Charlesworth
Pillar Box Lane, Hadlow,
Tonbridge, Kent TN11 9SW
Great Britain
Tel: +44 (0) 173 281 0081
www.downderry-nursery.co.uk.
info@downderry-nursery.co.uk

LE JARDIN DES ARÔMES
Collection of aromatic and scented plants grown around an old still.
Promenade de l'Eygues
26110 Nyons - France
Enquire at the Nyons tourist office about guided visits:
Place de la Libération
26110 Nyons - France
Tel: +33 (0) 4 75 26 10 35

LES JARDINS DE GAP-CHARANCE
Garden visits and workshops on a lavender theme: botany history and distillation.
Domaine de Charance
05000 Gap - France
For detailed recorded information:
Tel: +33 (0) 4 92 51 21 79

LES JARDINS DU PRIEURÉ
DE SALAGON
Medieval garden, medicinal
herb garden and scented
garden open to visitors.
Themed visits for a more
detailed understanding of
lavender. Distillation workshop
for children organized every
Wednesday in summer.
04300 Mane - France
Tel: +33 (0) 4 92 75 70 50 Fax:
+33 (0) 4 92 75 70 58
www.musee-de-salagon.com
info@musee-de-salagon.com

PÉPINIÈRE FILIPPI
Visitors to the collection
by appointment only. Over
60 varieties of lavender and
lavandin are on sale at the
nursery. Detailed catalogue
available.
Route Nationale 113
34140 Mèze - France
Tel: +33 (0)4 67 43 88 69
Fax: +33 (0)4 67 43 84 59
www.jardin-sec.com
olivier.filippi@wanadoo.fr

Buying lavender essences and flowers

A rough idea of retail prices:
10ml/⅜fl oz essential oil of
lavender augustifolia costs around
£5.50–£7.00, 10ml/⅜fl oz of
essential oil of lavandin between
£3 and £4. Spike lavender
essential oil starts from about
£4.50 for 10 ml/⅜fl oz.

BERNARD LAGET
This herbalist sells essential
oils from the region, sachets
of herbs for making teas and,
amongst his beauty products,
two wonderful foot creams with
a lavender base: walkers will
love them…
Place aux herbes
26170 Buis-les-Baronnies
France
Tel: +33 (0) 4 75 28 13 34
Fax: +33 (0) 4 75 28 13 34

FLORAME
In summer, just in front of the
charming shop belonging to the
Musée des Arômes, you can
take part in distillations of all
of the lavandin grown in nearby
gardens: it takes place, literally
on the doorstep, in the Cours
Mirabeauin the centre of the
town. The shop sells essential
oils, quality soaps, several
ranges of organic beauty
products and blends of oils for
putting in fragrance diffusers.
• 34, cours Mirabeau
13210 Saint-Rémy-de-Provence
France
Tel: +33 (0) 4 32 60 05 18
Fax: +33 (0) 4 32 92 48 80
• 18 et 8, rue Dupuytren
75006 Paris - France
Tel: +33 (0) 1 44 07 34 53
Available on the internet from:
www.florame.com

HERBORISTERIE CHAVASSIEU
Herbal shop classed as an
historic monument right in the
heart of Saint-Jean, the old
quarter of Lyon. A range of
Sanoflore products are available
as well as lavender teas.
8, place Saint-Jean
69002 Lyon - France
Tel/Fax: +33 (0) 4 78 37 88 18

HERBORISTERIE D'HIPPOCRATE
Nicole Sabardel is a pharmacist
who has chosen to sell herbs in
this small, welcoming, modern
shop. Lavender essential oil
and dried flowers can be
bought here.
42, rue Saint-André-des-Arts
75006 Paris - France
Tel: +33 (0) 1 40 51 87 03
Fax: +33 (0) 1 45 26 98 57

JEAN-PIERRE DUC
A professional lavender
culivator sells a variety of
lavender essential oils, lavandin
and lavandinex, with calming
and refreshing properties.
Ferme La Roberte
Quartier Carroir
26230 Grignan - France
Tel: +33 (0) 4 75 46 52 72

LABORATOIRE PRANARÔM
Wholesaler that sells essential
oils and lavender beauty products
to chemists, including bath oils
and lavender-based shampoo
for getting rid of lice, etc.
84123 Pertuis CEDEX - France
Tel: +33 (0) 4 90 09 36 80
Fax: +33 (0) 4 90 09 36 85

MAISON DES HUILES
ESSENTIELLES
Sells a good selection of
essential oils and blends for
diffusers, as well as beauty
products containing essential
oils and fine quality products.
04130 Volx - France
Tel: +33 (0) 4 92 78 46 77
Fax: +33 (0) 4 92 78 44 82

LE PETIT CHÊNE
Roselyne Dubois distils an
essential oil of incomparable
quality from wild lavender that
she gathers on the famous
Montagne de Lure.
Les Agreniers
04150 Banon - France
Tel: +33 (0) 4 92 73 27 56

SANOFLORE
This company located near the
Vercors National Park, combines
cultivating aromatic plants, and
distillation with the manufacture
of a range of beauty products,
which are all certified organic.
They have a lovely shop open in
summer, surrounded by a garden
of aromatic plants. Sanoflore
products are sold in Botanic
shops and a number of other
organic health and beauty shops.
26400 Gigors-et-Lozeron - France
Tel: +33 (0) 4 75 76 46 61
Fax: +33 (0) 4 75 76 46 38
Sanoflore will direct you to the
nearest supplier:
www.sanoflore.net

Beauty Products

L'ANTICA PROFUMERIA AL
SACRO CUORE
Sells Durance en Provence
products (for cleaning the

house, hygiene and body care).
Galleria Falcone Borsellino
40122 Bologna – Italy
Tel: + 390 (0) 51 23 52 11

L'ARAIGNÉE ROUGE
Sells Durance en Provence
products (for cleaning the
house, hygiene and body care).
7, place des eaux-vives
CH1207 Geneva – Switzerland
Tel/Fax: +41 (0)22 736 63 60

AROMAS DE PROVENZAS
Sells Durance en Provence
products (for cleaning the
house, hygiene and body care).
• Centre commercial
"La Esquina del Bernabéu"
Madrid – Spain
Tel: +34 (0) 91 619 63 23
• C/ Rambla del Prat, 13
Barcelona – Espagne
Tel: +34 (0) 93 218 35 54

LE CLOS D'AGUZON
From the land of the 'Super-
blue', you can purchase
essential oils, eau de toilettes,
scented candles and potpourris
from a large shop in the middle
of the countryside beside the
factory where they are made.
26170 Saint-Auban-sur-
l'Ouvèze - France
Tel: +33 (0) 4 75 28 64 99
Fax: +33 (0) 4 75 28 64 83
claire.reynier@closdaguzon.com

LES COMPTOIRS DE PROVENCE
These shops sell a complete
range of products for the home,
for use in the bath, etc., from
the Durance en Provence label.
• 40, rue Francis Davso
13001 Marseille - France
Tel/Fax: +33 (0) 4 91 33 52 47
• 24, rue Vignon
75009 Paris - France
Tel/Fax: +33 (0) 1 47 42 04 10

LE DOMAINE SAINT-QUENTIN
Yvonne Knowles has a wide
knowledge of lavender and sells
beauty products from Provence
and the USA.
35 NW 1st Street
Homestead, FL 33030 - USA

Tel: +1 (0) 305 245 1645
Fax: +1 (0) 305 245 1647
Also available over the internet
from: *dsqlavender@aol.com*

GUERLAIN
Two famous lavender perfumes
were created by Guerlain: Jicky
and l'Eau de Cologne du Coq…
• 68, avenue des Champs-Élysées
75008 Paris - France
Tel: +33 (0) 1 45 62 52 57
Fax: +33 (0) 1 40 74 09 91
Also available from various
branches of
• Boots
Tandem Retail Park
Colliers Wood
London SW19 2A2
Great Britain
Tel: +44 (0) 208 640 7506
And from
• Bloomingdale's 1000 Third Av
10022 New York - USA
Tel: +1 (0) 212 705 2792
A list of other Guerlain shops
and retailers can be found on
the internet at:
www.guerlain.fr

THE GREAT DAME
Sells Durance en Provence
products (for cleaning the
house, hygiene and body care).
105 Front St
Stratford Ontario
Canada N5A 4H1
Tel: +1 (0) 519 275 3787
Fax: +1 (0) 519 275 3582
thegreatdameshop@yahoo.ca

KAMI
Sells Durance en Provence
products (for cleaning the
house, hygiene and body care).
C.so Matteotti 42
10121 Turin - Italy
Tel: +39 (0) 11 95 31 262
Fax: +39 (0) 11 95 61 827

L'OCCITANE
You can visit the factory at
Manosque where products are
sold at factory shop prices and
find eau de colognes and
lavender vinegar… At the end
of August and in September,
products from the lavender

harvest arrive in all of the
l'Occitane shops; the bouquets
and beauty products creating a
lavender-blue display.
• ZI Saint-Maurice
04100 Manosque - France
Tel: +33 (0) 4 92 70 19 00
Fax: +33 (0) 4 92 87 34 23
The addresses of all of the
l'Occitane shops, in France and
throughout the world can be
found on their internet site:
www.loccitane.com

PARFUMERIE GÉNÉRALE
This shop sells lavender-based
products from all over the world.
6, rue Robert-Étienne
75008 Paris - France
Tel: +33 (0) 1 43 59 10 62
Fax: +33 (0) 1 43 59 10 63
Order over the internet from
the site:
www.parfumeriegenerale.com

PROVENCE-SCENTS
By combining orders (this is
a wholesaler) you can buy
from a fairly complete range of
products: syrups, preserves,
potpourris, flowers and
bouquets, essential oils, beauty
products, soaps and the
lavender dollies that are so
hard to find.
38, rue André-de-Richaud
84330 Caromb - France
Tel: +33 (0) 4 90 62 51 76
Fax: +33 (0) 4 90 62 36 36
info@provence-scents.fr
www.provence-scents.fr

REDCURRENT PONSONBY
Sells Durance en Provence
products (for cleaning the
house, hygiene and body care).
63 Ponsonby Road,
Ponsonby, Auckland
New Zealand
Tel: + 64 (0)93 61 10 03
redcurrent.ak@xtra.co.nz

SAVONNERIE ARTISANALE
DE LA TOUR DU GUET
Soap with lavender essential
oil.
04120 Castellane - France
Tel: +33 (0) 4 92 83 69 02

For the home

À POINT NOMMÉ
Sells a large selection of
embroidery kits with a lavender
motif. One of the loveliest
is drawn from a botanical
illustration of the different
species of lavender in the
world.
3, rue des Taules
26200 Montélimar - France
Tel: +33 (0) 4 75 51 04 58

LES ANNÉES CASSANDRE
Sault antiquarian, Lucien
Vakanas, collects old lavender
labels. He also sells antique
lavender eau de toilette
perfume bottles in his
antiques shop.
Avenue de la Résistance
84390 Sault - France
Tel: +33 (0) 4 90 64 11.66
Fax: +33 (0) 4 90 64 11 82

LE CHÂTEAU DE L'ANGE
Édith Mezard embroiders table
linen and bedlinen by hand
with lavender in mauve and
white. You can even order your
trousseau from her!
Lumières
84220 Goult - France
Tel: +33 (0) 4 90 72 36 41
Fax: +33 (0) 4 90 72 36 69

LE CHÂTEAU DE LA GABELLE
Marguerite Blanc makes
traditional round bouquets tied
with woven ears of wheat. In
the village, nearly all the houses
sell small bouquets.
26570 Ferrassières - France
Tel: +33 (0) 4 75 28 80 54
Fax: +33 (0) 4 75 28 85 56
www.chateau-la-gabelle.com

COOPÉRATIVE DE PRODUCTEURS
LOCAUX D'APT
Sells lavender flowers and
wheat for making your own
bouquets.
Rue de la République
84 390 Sault - France
Tel: +33 (0) 4 90 64 08 98

DYPTIQUE
Sells a wonderful lavender-
scented candle called
Feuilles de Lavande.
• 195, Westbourne grove
W11 2SB London
Great Britain
Tel: +44 (0) 207 727 8673
• 34, boulevard Saint-Germain
75005 Paris - France
Tel: +33 (0) 1 43 26 45 27
Fax: +33 (0) 1 43 54 27 01
www.dyptiqueparis.com

SANOFLORE
Lavender fragrance for the
home and organic scent to put
on your pillow to help you
sleep.
26400 Gigors-et-Lozeron
France
Tel: +33 (0) 4 75 76 46 61
Fax: +33 (0) 4 75 76 46 38
Order from the site:
www.sanoflore.net

TENTATION BRODERIES
Marvellous selection of
embroidery kits with lavender
motifs: bouquets, alphabet
samplers…
4, avenue du Général-de-Gaulle
84110 Vaison-la-Romaine
France
Tel: +33 (0) 4 90 28 82 77

Lavender delicacies

CONFISERIE ANDRÉ BOYER
Nougat with almonds from
Provence and lavender honey.
This pretty wood panelled
cake shop sells lavender-
flavoured boiled sweets,
lavender lemonade and
lavender cordial.
Rue de la Porte-des-Aires
84390 Sault
France
Tel: +33 (0) 4 90 64 00 23
Fax: +33 (0) 4 90 64 08 99

FROMAGERIE DU COMTAT
Hidden among the
exceptionally fine cheeses
produced by this reputable
establishment is the lavandine

du Venaissin, created by
Claudine Vigier.
23, Place de l'Hôtel-de-Ville
84200 Carpentras - France
Tel: +33 (0) 4 90 60 00 17
Fax: +33 (0) 4 90 60 41 05

FROMAGERIE LOU CANESTEOU
Josiane Déal, who received the
award for best worker in France
2004, sells lavender-flavoured
goats' cheese.
10, rue Raspail
84110 Vaison-la-Romaine
France
Tel: +33 (0) 4 90 28 79 22
Fax: +33 (0) 4 90 28 79 33

GOUMANYAT
In his retail shop, Jean-Marie
Thiercelin, spice wholesaler,
sells lavender oil infused with
lavender and lemon thyme,
lavender honey and teas, as well
as crystallised lavender and
lavender essence for cooking.
3, rue Dupuis
75003 Paris - France
Tel: +33 (0) 1 44 78 96 74
Fax: +33 (0) 1 44 78 96 75
www.goumanyat.com
contact@goumanyat.com

LINDA STRADLEY
Sells lavender and recipes for
culinary use on the internet site:
whatscookingamerica.net

NEW TREE
Lavender milk chocolates made
by Belgian pastry chef Pierre
Marcolini. Available in Botanic
shops:
Tel: +33 (0) 4 50 31 27 00
Fax: +33 (0) 4 50 31 27 01
Botanic shops in France and
Italy listed on the site:
www.botanic.com
info@botanic.com

PÂTISSERIE ANDRÉ SUBE
Famous lavender chocolates,
pêche de vigne and lavender
sorbet and lavender ice cream.
2, rue de la République
84110 Vaison-la-Romaine
France
Tel: +33 (0) 4 90 36 06 75

LE RUCHER
Max Laugier, apiculturist, sells
lavender honey… It's real
nectar: each hive only produces
9½lbs of honey! Postal orders
taken.
Les Grandes Aires
04210 Valensole
France
Tel: +33 (0) 4 92 74 91 89

Restaurants

LA BONNE ÉTAPE
Jany Gleize offers a menu
entirely dedicated to lavender:
Terrine of local game with
lavender, duck, lavender
honey ice cream, etc.
Chemin du lac
04160 Château-Arnoux
France
Tel: +33 (0) 4 92 64 00 09
Fax: +33 (0) 4 92 64 37 36
bonneetape@relaischateaux.com

DOMINIQUE BUCAILLE
Offers a menu entirely
dedicated to lavender.
43, boulevard des tilleuls
04800 Manosque - France
Tel/Fax: +33 (0) 4 92 72 32 28

HOSTELLERIE DU VAL DE SAULT
Yves Gattechaud offers a menu
entirely dedicated to lavender.
Some of his recipes appear in
this book.
Route de Saint-Trinité
84390 Sault - France
Tel: +33 (0) 4 90 64 01 41
Fax: +33 (0) 4 92 64 12 74
www.valdesault.com
valdesault@aol.com

LE RELAIS DE L'EMPEREUR
The hotel barman, Henri
Revol, invented a cocktail
called Couleur Lavande.
Although the exact recipe is
secret, it is believed to be made
of gin and lemon juice with
lavender and violet cordials…
26200 Montélimar - France
Tel: +33 (0) 4 75 01 29 00
Fax: +33 (0) 4 75 01 32 21

Lavender festivals

CEREMONIES OF THE
COMMANDERIE DE LA LAVANDE
FINE DE HAUTE PROVENCE
During the summer festivals,
the head of this association
inducts lavender lovers who
swear loyalty to the flower in
highly colourful ceremonies.
26570 Ferrassières
Tel: +33 (0) 4 75 28 81 21

LAVENDER PROCESSION
AT DIGNE-LES-BAINS
Procession of floats decorated
with lavender. Agricultural fair.
Last weekend in July and first
weekend in August.
Contact the tourist office:
Le Rond-Point
04000 Digne-les-Bains
France
Tel: +33 (0) 4 92 36 62 62
Fax: +33 (0) 4 92 32 27 24

EXPOSITION À MONTÉLIMAR
A beautiful lavender exhibition
set under the shady trees of the
park in the middle of the town:
woven dollies, embroidery,
lavender and lavendin plants,
perfumes, cosmetics, lavender
delicacies. Tasting of the bleu-
lavande aperitif, made in
Montélimar.
Second weekend in July.
Contact the tourist office:
Les Allées Provençales
Avenue Rochemaure
26200 Montélimar - France
Tel: +33 (0) 4 75 01 00 20
Fax: +33 (0) 4 75 52 33 69

FESTIVAL DU JARDIN DU SOLEIL
The Jardin du Soleil organic
farm organizes a lavender
festival every third weekend in
July, which brings together the
eight producers in the Sequim
area.
3932 Sequim Dungeness Way
Sequim, WA 98382 - USA
Tel: +1 (0) 877 527 3461
www.jardindusoleil.com
lavender@jardindusoleil.com

WILLOW POND FARM FESTIVAL
A lavender festival is held in
June every year at this farm,
which grows organic aromatic
plants. Garden visits. Lavender
infusions, bouquets, cosmetics,
etc. for sale.
145, tract road
Fairfield. PA 17320 - USA
Tel/Fax: +1 (0) 717 642 6387
info@willowpondherbs.com
www.willowpondherbs.com

FÊTE DE LA LAVANDE À SAULT
Distillation by a portable still.
15 August
Contact the tourist office:
Avenue Promenade
84390 Sault - France
Tel: +33 (0) 4 90 64 01 21
Fax: +33 (0) 4 90 64 15 03

FOIRE PAYSANNE
À FERRASSIÈRES
Country fair with a working
display of a small mobile still.
Sale of lavender flowers,
bouquets, lavender honey and
local speciality produce.
Demonstration of lavender
cutting.
First weekend in July.
Contact the tourist office:
L'Autin
26570 Montbrun-les-Bains
France
Tel: +33 (0) 4 75 28 82 49
Fax: +33 (0) 4 75 28 82 98

Bibliography

Bonnefoy, Jean-Paul, *La Lavande*, Barthélemy, 1997.

Bouvier, Jean, *Célébration de la lavande*, Robert Morel, 1966.

Cossalter, Élisabeth, *Lavandes, brins de Provence*, Didier Richard, 1993.

Etcheverria, Olivier, *La Lavande : dix façons de la préparer*, Éditions de l'Épure, 2002.

Everlegh, Tessa, *Lavender, Practical inspirations for natural gifts, country craft*, Lorenz Books, 1996.

Fabiani, Gilbert, *Mémoires de la lavande*, Équinoxe, 1999.

Giono, Jean, "La lavande est l'âme de la haute Provence", in *Provence*, Gallimard, 1993
   (First published in February 1958 in the perfume maker's magazine: *La France et ses parfums*).

Genus lavandula, Royal Botanic Gardens, Kew, 2004.

Meunier Christiane, *Lavande et lavandins*, Édisud, 1985.

Mourre, Charles, *La Lavande française, sa culture, son industrie, son analyse*, Gauthier-Villars, 1923.

Roubin, Lucienne, *Le Monde des odeurs*, Meridiens Klincksieck, 1989.

Silvester, Hans, *Lavender, fragrance of Provence*, trans Meunier, Harry N Abrams, 1996.

Silvester, Hans, *Provence, Terre de lavandes*, La Martinière, 1995.

Valnet, Docteur, *The practice of Aromatherapy*, Healing Arts Press, 1990.

Valnet, Docteur, *Aromathérapie, traitement des maladies par les essences de plantes*, Librairie Maloine, 1964.

Credits

The author would like to thank Rodolphe Baltz, aromatherapist and founder of Sanoflore; Marguerite Blanc, for her boundless kindness and lovely bouquets; Sabrina da Conceicao, who helped me explore the hilltop villages of the Haute-Provence Alps and of the Montagne de Lure; Roselyne Dubois, distiller and wild lavender picker; Bernard Ducros, for harvesting wild lavender and for finding a small antique still that remains in use today; Olivier Filippi, for his introduction to the diverse varieties of lavender created by gardeners throughout the world; Élisabeth Hauwuy, who created the Lavender Routes, and to her team, for giving access to their archives and useful contacts; Yvonne Knowles, of the Domaine Saint-Quentin, found the extract from *The Arabian Nights* with which this book opens; Bernard Laget, who gave access to his antique collection of lavender postcards; Sébastien Mesnières, for the guided tour of Mévouillon's 'Super-blue'; Danielle Musset, curator of the Musée de Salagon in Mane, who gave me access to its archives; Brigitte Naviner, who tracked down the full text of Giono's article "Lavender is the Soul of Haute Provence" in an old perfume-maker's review and discussed ideas about the project; Jeanne-Marie Pascal, for an afternoon of botany and plant collection on the theme of lavander; Nicole Sabardel, chemist and herbalist; Philippe Soguel, for explaining distillation; Lucien Vakanas, antiquarian in Sault.

Thanks also to Bénédicte Appels, Claude Broquin, Yves Gattechaud, André Sube, Claudine Vigier, who kindly agreed to share their lavender recipes.

Thanks to Émilie Lézénès, and Annick Goutal, Alexandre Turpault, Descamps, Kitchen bazaar, Origin's and Sanoflore.

Picture credits

All photographs by Sophie Boussahba, apart from:
Archipel-studio: pp36–7, 73; Bridgeman: p119 (Bibliothèque nationale de France, Archives Charmet); Corbis: pp8–9 (Hulton-Deutsch Collection), 10a, 11 (Blue Lantern Studio), *22* (Hulton-Deutsch Collection), 68–69a (Bryn Colton, Assignments Photographers); Getty: pp68–9b (Robert Harding World Imagery); Hoa-qui: p16 (Manfred Gottschalk), 43 (Emmanuel Valentin), 44–5 (G. Martin-Raget); Lamontagne: pp63a, 67a, 70 b, 71 b, 72, 77, 80–81, 83b ; Mary Evans Picture Library: pp62, 129, 131; Mise-au-Point: pp65, 74–5, 78-79 (Arnaud Descat), 83a (F. Strauss); B and P Perdereau: p76; Rapho: p46 (Hans Silvester); Roger-Viollet: p120; Scope: p47 (Jacques Guillard).